Praise for *Winning Togetl*

'Work relationships that don't work make everybody miserable. But for the world-weary post-Covid, it can be hard to find the energy to tackle them. Cue this wonderful book from a seasoned team of experts, which shows you how. In an accessible format with practical advice and exercises, this book takes you by the hand and walks you through next steps. I hope it will be on everyone's desk in the future.'

Dr Eve Poole, OBE, author of
Leadersmithing

'This is such a useful resource for working relationships, particularly in this new hybrid world of work. From navigating relationships in online meetings to building trust with colleagues, I've already put into practice many of the super practical tips and tricks contained in this book.'

Jessica Bradford, Digital Communications
Manager, BT Global

'This excellent book comes along at the perfect moment, when navigating the post -pandemic "new normal" requires superb skills in communication to build trust and achieve resilient, lastingly great relationships. The authors have curated this practical handbook, complete with simple and thought provoking exercises to try on your own and with your teams. Whether you read it cover-to-cover or cherry pick the chapters that speak directly to your current situation, use it to understand and refine your own personal powers of communication to turn obstacles into teaching moments of healthy conflict and people problem solving. Highly enjoyable and instantly effective!"

Dina Dommett, Dean of Ashridge Hult International
Business School

'I have been impressed by the practical nature of this book. Patricia, Fiona and Viki (academics and practitioners) provide useful tips, exercises and frameworks for working together with others. The book is easy to read and covers key qualities and skills for a post-covid changing workplace including how to create trust, influence others and increase emotional intelligence as well as how to become more agile in your relationships with others. The book can be your guide when preparing for a high stakes team meeting, handling messy team dynamics and/or in support for finding a better work/life balance. I strongly recommend this book. It will help you achieve both individual and team goals.'

Guy Lubitsh, Professor in Leadership and Psychology

'This book takes the well-worn challenges we all find in building and maintaining good working relationships and applies them to the new world of work. Through its useful exercises, checklists and actionable examples it pulls together lessons for us all, whether people manager, colleague, partner or friend. It's refreshing to find a book backed by academic research and insight but written in such a simple and accessible way. I found the FAQs and authors' suggestions on how they would tackle these challenges particularly useful. In today's fast-changing and complex world of work, it's true to say that *Winning Together* is the only route to success!'

Siân Harrington, co-founder and editorial director at The People Space; founder director at Reignite HR

Winning Together

Pearson

The Financial Times

Winning Together

The secrets of better work relationships

Patricia Hind, Fiona Elsa Dent
and Viki Holton

Pearson

Harlow, England • London • New York • Boston • San Francisco • Toronto • Sydney
Dubai • Singapore • Hong Kong • Tokyo • Seoul • Taipei • New Delhi
Cape Town • São Paulo • Mexico City • Madrid • Amsterdam • Munich • Paris • Milan

PEARSON EDUCATION LIMITED
KAO Two
KAO Park
Harlow CM17 9NA
United Kingdom
Tel: +44 (0)1279 623623
Web: www.pearson.com

First edition published 2023 (print and electronic)

ISBN: 978-1-292-42122-3 (print)
         978-1-292-42123-0 (ePub)

British Library Cataloguing-in-Publication Data
A catalogue record for the print edition is available from the British Library

Library of Congress Cataloging-in-Publication Data
A catalog record for the print edition is available from the Library of Congress

10 9 8 7 6 5 4 3 2 1
27 26 25 24 23

Cover design by Two Associates

Print edition typeset in 10/14 Charter ITC Pro by Straive
Printed by Ashford Colour Press Ltd, Gosport

NOTE THAT ANY PAGE CROSS REFERENCES REFER TO THE PRINT EDITION

Contents

Contents

Pearson's Commitment to Diversity, Equity and Inclusion

Pearson is dedicated to creating bias-free content that reflects the diversity, depth and breadth of all learners' lived experiences. We embrace the many dimensions of diversity including, but not limited to, race, ethnicity, gender, sex, sexual orientation, socioeconomic status, ability, age and religious or political beliefs.

Education is a powerful force for equity and change in our world. It has the potential to deliver opportunities that improve lives and enable economic mobility. As we work with authors to create content for every product and service, we acknowledge our responsibility to demonstrate inclusivity and incorporate diverse scholarship so that everyone can achieve their potential through learning. As the world's leading learning company, we have a duty to help drive change and live up to our purpose to help more people create a better life for themselves and to create a better world.

Our ambition is to purposefully contribute to a world where:

- Everyone has an equitable and lifelong opportunity to succeed through learning.
- Our educational products and services are inclusive and represent the rich diversity of learners.
- Our educational content accurately reflects the histories and lived experiences of the learners we serve.
- Our educational content prompts deeper discussions with students and motivates them to expand their own learning and worldview.

We are also committed to providing products that are fully accessible to all learners. As per Pearson's guidelines for accessible educational Web media, we test and retest the capabilities of our products against the highest standards for every release, following the WCAG guidelines in developing new products for copyright year 2022 and beyond. You can learn more about Pearson's commitment to accessibility at:

https://www.pearson.com/us/accessibility.html

While we work hard to present unbiased, fully accessible content, we want to hear from you about any concerns or needs regarding this Pearson product so that we can investigate and address them.

- Please contact us with concerns about any potential bias at: https://www.pearson.com/report-bias.html

- For accessibility-related issues, such as using assistive technology with Pearson products, alternative text requests, or accessibility documentation, email the Pearson Disability Support team at: disability.support@pearson.com

Acknowledgements

This book is a distillation of our collective experience of working with individuals and teams at all levels in organisations from many different national and international sectors, varied backgrounds and in a wide range of roles. Our sincere thanks go to all those with whom we have had working relationships during our own careers. These people – colleagues, bosses, team members, board members, clients, coachees and participants on our many courses – have helped us to formulate our ideas about building successful working relationships. Without their contribution and input *Winning Together* may not have happened.

Publisher's acknowledgements

1 C. JoyBell: Quoted by C. Joy Bell; 11 Patrick Bird: Adapted from The ARC of Distortion, Patrick Bird https://www.projectsmart.co.uk/communications-management/the-arc-of-distortion.php; 15 Hugh Mackay: Quoted by Hugh Mackay; 29 and 64 Bill Gates: Quoted by Bill Gates; 34 Rahul Guha: Quoted by Rahul Guha; 36 Alexandra Shulman: Quoted by Alexandra Shulman; 41 Joan Chandos Baez: Quoted by Joan Baez; 46 Management Pocketbooks: Dent, F. (2009) The Working Relationships Pocketbook. Copyright (C) Management Pocketbooks. Used by Permission; 56 Pearson Education Limited: Sue Hadfield, Gill Hasson (2009) Bounce: Use the Power of Resilience to Live the Life You Want, Pearson Education Limited; 57 Harvard Business Publishing: Harvard Business Review on Building Personal and Organizational Resilience (Harvard Business Review Paperback Series), Harvard Business Press; 64 Joanne Rowling: Quoted by J K Rowling; 64 Bill Gates: Quoted by Bill Gates; 64 Oprah Gail Winfrey: Quoted by Oprah Winfrey; 64 and 199 Confucius: Quoted by Confucius; 65 John Williams: Quoted by John Williams; 69 Penguin Random House: Sir Richard Branson (2008), Business Stripped Bare Adventures of a Global Entrepreneur, Virgin Books; 83 Penguin Random House: Daniel Goleman (1995) Emotional Intelligence' (EI) , Bantam Books, Inc.; 84 Bantam Books, Inc.: Adapted from Goleman, D. (1995). Emotional intelligence. Bantam Books, Inc.; 93 Lee Bo-young: Quoted by Bo Young Lee; 96 Emerald

Publishing Limited: Adapted from Kim, W. C. and Mauborgne, R. (2005) 'Value innovation: a leap into the blue ocean', Emerald Group Publishing Limited/*Journal of Business Research*, Volume 26, Issue 4; **98 Aristotle:** Quoted by Aristotle; **107 Deepak Chopra:** Quoted by Deepak Chopra; **109 Pearson Education Limited:** Adapted from Brent, M. and Dent, F.E. (2014) The Leaders Guide to Managing People: How to use soft skills to get hard results. FT Publishing; **130 Pearson Education Limited:** Brent, Mike, Dent, Fiona, *Leader's Guide to Managing People*, 1st edition, ©2014. Reprinted by permission of Pearson Education Limited; **135 Maya Angelou:** Quoted by Maya Angelou; **147 Seth Godin:** Quoted by Seth Godin; **149 David Joseph Bohm:** Quoted by David Bohm; **153 Rachel Naomi Remen:** Quoted by Rachel Remen; **158 Crown Business:** Based on Senge, P. M. (2014). The fifth discipline fieldbook: Strategies and tools for building a learning organization. Crown Business; **163 Marcus Buckingham:** Quoted by Marcus Buckingham; **169 Simmons University:** Rivera-Beckstrom, A. & Van Dam, E. (2021) The Importance of Authenticity in the Workplace: The 2021 Leadership Development Survey. Simmons University Institute for Inclusive Leadership; **173 Chris Patten:** Quoted by Lord Chris Patten; **177 Mahatma Gandhi:** Quoted by Mahatma Gandhi; **189 Gerard Manley Hopkins:** Quoted by Gerard Manley Hopkins; **195 Dana Gionta:** Quoted by Dana Gionta; **207 Hilary Devey:** Quoted by Hilary Devey.

About the authors

Patricia Hind, Professor of Management and Leadership Development BSc, MSc, PhD, AFBPS

Patricia is Professor of Management and Leadership Development at Ashridge Executive Education at Hult International Business School. Her career has taken her from researching in the House of Commons, to the Financial Services sector for several years and then into Higher Education. A Chartered Organisational and Business Psychologist she held posts at the Universities of Sheffield, Leeds and City University in London before joining Ashridge Executive Education. Her expertise is in Leadership Development and Management Learning, and as Director of the Centre for Research in Executive Development she gained wide-ranging experience of helping national and global clients to develop their leaders for organisational and personal success. She is an independent university governor and her consultancy offers both personal and organisational development services, specialising in self-awareness, relational leadership and moving organisational cultures towards sustainability.

Patricia's work focusses on the personal and contextual aspects of leading. She believes strongly in the importance of building sustainable, successful organisations through developing skilled, confident and resilient leadership at all levels in the organisation. Patricia's clients particularly value her thoughtful expertise which is delivered lightly and her ability to link knowledge and theory to real-life practicality.

Patricia is an Associate Fellow of the British Psychological Society, a Justice of the Peace, a Freeman of the City of London and a Visiting Research Fellow at the University of Stellenbosch in South Africa. Her first degree is in Psychology from Leeds University, her MSc is in Industrial/Organisational Psychology from the University of Hull and she holds a PhD from the University of Leeds which examined the complexities of 'Managing and Motivating Volunteers'. Patricia has published widely in both professional and peer reviewed journals and has authored three books while contributing to many national and international conferences. She is qualified to use a wide range of psychometric instruments and her teaching and research interests include Leadership, Sustainability, Diversity and Inclusion, Managing Virtual Relationships, Resilience and Career Agility.

Fiona Elsa Dent MSc, MA

Fiona is a Professor of Practice for Ashridge Executive Education at Hult International Business School, an independent management trainer, executive coach and author. Previously she was a Director of Executive Education at Ashridge and a member of the Ashridge Leadership Team where she was responsible for one of the two education faculty groups that managed programmes, client relationships and delivered management development solutions across Ashridge. Fiona was also involved with her colleagues in setting the strategic direction of the organisation with a particular focus on human resources. She has also worked in the financial services industry, local and central government.

Fiona has Programme and Client Director experience, and has worked with a range of organisations and clients on a national and international basis. Recent clients include the BBC, NHS, easyJet, Abu Dhabi Executive Council, St Gobain and Novartis Pharmaceuticals. Fiona teaches and consults in a broad spectrum of leadership, personal, interpersonal and relationship skills and is trained in a range of psychometrics. Recent coaching clients include a range of Senior Civil Servants, medical and management personnel in the NHS and a Senior Manager in the tourism industry.

Fiona has co-authored a range of books including: *When Teams Work: How to develop and lead a high-performing team* (FT Publishing 2022), *Career Agility: Strategies For Success* (Cambridge Scholars Publishing 2020), *The Leadership of Teams* (Bloomsbury 2017), *Thrive and Survive as a Working Woman: Your Coaching Toolkit* (Bloomsbury 2016), *The Leader's Guide to Coaching and Mentoring: How to use soft skills to get hard results* (Pearson 2015), *The Leader's Guide to Managing People: How to use soft skills to get hard results* (Pearson 2014), *Women in Business: Navigating Career Success* (Palgrave 2012), *The Leader's Guide to Influence: How to use soft skills to get hard results* (Pearson 2010), *Working Relationships Pocketbook (Management Pocketbooks Ltd 2009), Influencing: Skills and Techniques for Business Success* (Palgrave Macmillan 2006), *The Leadership Pocketbook* (Management Pocketbooks Ltd 2003).

Viki Holton is Adjunct Research Fellow at Ashridge Executive Education at Hult International Business School. She was a member of the Ashridge Centre for Business and Society and involved as a Board member for EWMD, the European Women's Management Development Network. She also edited the EWMD Newsletter for a number of years.

Viki's research and writing interests include teams, career management, leadership generally as well as women leaders with a keen interest in the topic of diversity and inclusion. She has co-authored a number of articles, chapters and books including *Career Agility: Strategies for success* (Cambridge Scholars Publishing 2020), Ego, Eco and Intuitive Leadership: A New Logic (Ashridge 2019), *How to Thrive and Survive as a Working Woman: Your coach yourself toolkit* (Bloomsbury 2016), *Women in Business: Navigating career success* (Palgrave 2012) as well as *How to Coach your Team: Release team potential and hit peak performance* (Pearson Books 2016).

Together with Patricia Hind she has published 'The Changing Nature of Leadership: Looking at the impact of social media (2019)' and in 2016 'Searching for the Holy Grail: Four principles of effective management development'.

Introduction

In every business, factory, office and working space you are likely to find some great relationships: people who work well together, as well as teams that are brilliantly successful in terms of cooperation and collaboration. The key qualities and skills that you need to ensure you can be part of this amazing world are contained in this book which will provide you with a practical toolkit to help you better understand how to build trust with others and to create outstanding work relationships.

Whether you are looking for a refresher course on improving your communication skills or for a new angle that might help you to resolve some blocks and challenges you are currently facing regarding your work relationships, this book can help you.

Understanding and improving your work relationship skills will turn a good manager into an outstanding one and transform a mediocre team into one of the best. We have worked with and coached many individuals over the years, and it can be a truly amazing change when people appreciate how to use these skills. Using our collective knowledge and expertise, we have distilled the many secrets we impart when teaching, coaching and consulting. Our aim is to help you with the tough stuff in developing powerful, successful working relationships. Not only do we introduce ideas, tips and techniques but we also suggest many reflective processes to help you to build new depth in your skill set.

Some people – and we can probably all think of examples around us currently or in previous places we have worked – are known to openly boast that, 'I really don't get the people stuff, but I do understand the A, B, C of delivering business results'. As if this excuses them for 'behaving like a bull in a china shop!'. There was one politician for instance who, although well known to the outside world as a superb diplomat, never bothered to exercise the same level of care and attention within their own team. In fact, shouting and temper tantrums as well as throwing items across the office were regular occurrences. All the worst aspects of a diva. There also are individuals who have spent too many years without any appreciation of how destructive their behaviour can be to those around them. Do you know a colleague who no one wants to upset because of the fuss and bother they will create? Or a toxic person who can spend days in a bad temper until they get their own way? Have you ever worked for a bully? These are all signs of people behaving badly and of a type of myopia, as they do not understand the power of cooperation and the potential personal synergy can offer any business.

One senior manager we know only had his epiphany moment when his boss compared him to a sailing ship, saying that although it looked at first glance as if he was gliding smoothly through the water, he should take the time to look behind him. He would then be aware of all the damage he did to others in order to achieve what he wanted: damage that other colleagues, and his boss, had to step in and resolve to reinstate a good working environment.

The best way to describe this book is to think of it like an excellent map or the best sat nav you can use by offering you ideas to journey in new directions. By the end of the book you will learn more about yourself, working with others and how you can create a more positive work environment. Essentially, it will provide you with details of how you can become the kind of leader or colleague that people love to have on their side: someone who is effective at communicating with others, efficient at networking and building support with key sponsors, thoughtful about others around them and also someone who delivers great results.

Often when deciding the key training initiatives for the business over the next 12–18 months, the focus veers towards topics such as finance and strategy, marketing and change management. However, while any and all of these do have a place in keeping skills at the leading edge, what is most important are the relationship and leadership skills, communication, influencing and topics such as performance through people. Perhaps we can illustrate this with an example. Think of an employer where, although there is a great razzamatazz on the company's values which include 'respect for people', in reality it is often completely the opposite for those people working there. Invariably when you talk to staff in such organisations, they will identify many ways that the business fails to maximise its potential. Not least there are stories about dysfunctional teams, departments or divisions where the day-to-day work relationships are rarely about great people skills and more about poor performance and individuals overloaded with too much work, too many unachievable deadlines and little support from their boss or co-workers. A bad boss, bullying and lack of respect for others are frequently encountered.

The secret ingredient in this book is debunking the myth that abounds in many organisations and professions that the 'people stuff' and relationship skills are soft, fluffy, not as important for business success and easier to develop than the harder skills of finance, marketing and strategy. In fact, relationship skills are tricky and essential and will be your superpower.

How to use this book

This book has been written with a strong focus on practical rather than academic information. Our aim is to provide you with a real-world guide to relationships at work, something that will be useful for everyone. While we do refer to some academic research, this is not our main focus. Early on we cover general issues about relationships at work and why they matter. We then offer you a toolkit of different topics: techniques and approaches to help you understand the things that will make a difference and contribute to excellence and success. Each chapter features concepts, ideas, tips, suggestions and practical exercises throughout to help you reflect, review and develop different aspects of your relationship skillset.

This book will be equally helpful if you read it from beginning to end or if you prefer to use it as a dip in dip out text. We hope you find it useful and informative.

chapter 1

Navigating the new normal for your work relationships?

'The only way that we can live, is if we grow. The only way that we can grow is if we change. The only way that we can change is if we learn. The only way we can learn is if we are exposed. And the only way that we can become exposed is if we throw ourselves out into the open. Do it. Throw yourself.'

C. Joy Bell, author

What do we mean by the 'new normal'? Since the worldwide Covid-19 pandemic, many of us have witnessed and experienced major changes in the way we work. In addition, for some, our attitude to work has been significantly altered.

In this chapter we will focus on the changes resulting from the new ways of working, the impact of the changes and the importance of three key skills for good working relationships: communication, trust and mutual respect.

Before the pandemic, the choice of how, when and with whom to work was enjoyed mostly by a small number of tech-savvy professionals. These individuals had high job choice, could work on their laptops from the Maldives and hop from one short-term contract to another. This was the stuff of LinkedIn posting (or boasting!).

Now we have a new reality. It's called 'hybrid work' and it's no longer a matter of preference for the few lucky ones, but a necessity for most industries and employees. This development is not of course due simply to Covid-19, but the pandemic accelerated a shift that began decades ago as we became used to technology, particularly, the internet, changing our lives and the way we communicate with each other. These changes had already had a profound impact on all aspects of business, from strategic issues such as expanding markets to the micromanagement of performance management and the recording of information.

Most organisations have taken significant steps to adjust to this evolving business landscape and those steps have been in two tandem directions. Firstly, for organisations to provide the flexibility, agility and resources needed, they have had to get the technology right. Major investment has, and still is, taking place, accompanied by disinvestment in physical space. Secondly, the culture for a dynamic working environment needs to be rethought, crafted and led. There is no doubt that our ability to work and meet remotely and still meet our targets has been a revelation to many businesses. Many of us have relished the freedom and flexibility that the new ways of working have brought. We are enjoying more autonomy but equally undoubtedly there have been flipsides. Many staff have felt isolated, some have never met their workmates and may never have worked in a physical office. Network opportunities are limited if not non-existent; team working and creativity can no longer be spontaneous; and all the relationships associated with our working lives are consequently becoming subtly different.

The reality of hybrid working means more organisations giving staff the opportunity to work both from home and the office, supported by ever more efficient and functional technology. This provides the opportunity for our working environments to be more personalised and allows employees to work in a way that makes sense for them and their own circumstances. But this comes at a price, and that price is personal connections between people, direct face-to-face communications and a blurring of the lines between home and work.

This is a hugely significant issue – most of us spend a great deal of our lives in our working environment and the quality of our relationships affects our productivity, our career progression, our enjoyment and indeed our health.

Take a moment to think about what these changes have meant to you. Use the box below to capture your thoughts about how your working life has changed or is changing in the new hybrid world. Do you like the flexibility? Do you miss the structure? Do you love being able to work in your track suit? Do you miss the water cooler chats? Do you feel more or less supported?

Try to be balanced – think about the things you really like as well as the things that perhaps frustrate you.

Hybrid working

What has changed for me	Things I like	Things I don't like

We are going to explore what these changes mean for your relationships at work and help you to understand why it is important that your relationships are positive, and how to develop them skilfully and maintain them in our new working reality.

First let's be clear – what do we mean by work relationships? Well, it's really all the interactions and connections you have with other people. Some will be closer than others, and easier to define than others, but you have a relationship with anybody who can influence the way you work, or conversely, with anybody that you can influence.

Some reasons for building good relationships at work are to do with how effective you are doing your job and contributing to the business. These would be things like:

- Improving collaboration and teamworking. If you have good rapport with others when, for example, working together on a project, you are more likely to share ideas, to be clear on what you are supposed to do and generally communicate better, which is likely to get a better result for the project. This is also helpful for sharing experience and developing each other's skill sets, which ultimately is good for the business.

- Improving your own productivity. If you are comfortable with the other people who work around you, you can concentrate better, can work harder and will be more likely to seek help and advice when you need it.

- Having good relationships with those around you at work can help you to be more creative. Feeling comfortable and trusting those you work with allows you to think laterally and 'out of the box' without worrying about whether people will think your ideas are foolish or naïve. Support and encouragement, along with openness to change, will enhance innovation and new ways of doing things, which leads to the flexibility and agility needed by many businesses today.

- Positive relationships within a team make it a welcoming and warm environment to work in. When there is no need for defensiveness or protecting one's 'patch', new members can integrate well, and will want to stay, thereby improving retention and minimising expensive recruitment costs.

Some other reasons for ensuring you have good working relationships are a lot more personal. These include fundamentally important things like:

- Increasing your morale. If you look forward to going into work because you enjoy working with the people there, you will find it easier to engage with your role and take pleasure in it – with a likely increase in your job satisfaction.

- Career progression – we may not like office politics, but we all acknowledge the importance of establishing good relationships with senior people in our organisation. Making sure that they appreciate you and the value you bring is much easier if you have good two-way interactions with them.

- Your psychological and physical health is affected significantly by your working life and much research has shown the dangers of poor relationships at work. The anxiety and stress caused by interpersonal difficulties has been associated with many serious health issues from heart conditions to depression. It is much easier to acknowledge these problems now than it used to be, and their importance cannot be underestimated.

The relationships we have mentioned so far are pretty much 'direct' and by that we mean that they take place in the working environment. However, there are other relationships that are equally relevant, but a bit more indirect. In this category we can include:

- Your immediate family. How things are at home has a huge impact on your working life. If you have worries about parents, children or partners these anxieties will inevitably 'leak' into your job. Many of us try to keep the two spheres very separate and guard our home privacy fiercely, and this has been made much more difficult by the advance of virtual and home working. Relationships with families may have been strained due to lack of space, lack of technology or simply lack of privacy, with consequences both for our bonds with our loved ones and for our jobs.

- Your friendship group is as much a part of your life as your family. Many of us find that our friends are drawn from similar types of employment – we may have trained together for example, or simply got to know each other at work and acquaintanceship has turned into friendship. Our friends are often our first port of call when we want to share concerns and our relationship with them provides a vital channel for sharing confidences, frustrations and ambitions.

- Your local community is also relevant, and perhaps more so than ever in our new reality. Many of us have taken to using our local coffee shop as a part-time office – our regular server will know how we like our lattes! We may have been engaged with community volunteering projects or taken up new hobbies, all of which create a network of relationships within which we engage with our new working reality.

What do we need to do differently to make sure we reap all benefits of hybrid working, and avoid its pitfalls? Undoubtedly, we need to keep our core relationship skills of listening empathically, asking good questions and applying our emotional intelligence, but what do we need to do to develop these skills so that they are still fit for purpose? And are there new skills that we need to define and learn? This book will help you to find the answers to these questions and provide you with the opportunity to proactively manage your relationships at work so that they are both positive and productive.

Let's start by exploring your own situation. Start by making a list below of all the relationships that are relevant to your working life.

You might want to include your boss, your direct reports, your peers and colleagues, your immediate family, your friendship group, your local community. Feel free to add anybody else who is relevant. You can have as many as you like.

Relationships important to my working life

1

2

3

4

5

6

7

8

9

10

Now you need to think about what, if anything, has changed or is changing in that relationship in relation to your work. Keep a very open mind and be as candid as you can be – nobody else will see this! Below is a table giving you some idea of the sort of thing you might come up with. This is followed by an empty table, which you can put your own experiences in. This exercise is a very personal self-reflection, so please be as honest as possible – it will help you to get the very most out of the book.

Relationship	Changes in the new working reality
My boss	I see much less of her; we don't get the chance to have an informal coffee unless we book it in the diary weeks ahead.
My team	The weekly catch-ups are a bit stilted – it's always 'the usual suspects' who take up all the airtime. I don't feel as connected to them and it's difficult to manage it online.
My children	They love having me home more, are getting used to me being 'at work' even though I'm in the kitchen.
My partner	Hates me nipping out to answer emails at 9.30 pm.
My mates and friends	Love having a chat at any time – except the ones who've been furloughed and are fed up.

Your relationship networks

Relationship	Changes in the new working reality

Those changes will be a mixture of good things and things that are less good. But all changes can be managed and any negative consequences can be mitigated, so we're going to think about how to turn them to your relational advantage wherever possible.

It will be helpful here if we remind ourselves of the important generic set of skills that make relationships work well in any circumstances. The strength of our relationship building, and management skills determines how well we negotiate, influence and work with others. All successful relationships are built on trust, respect and understanding. This will not be new to you, but a refresher about how to ensure those conditions are present is always useful!

Fundamentals for good working relationships

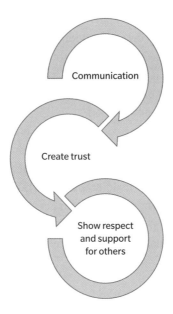

Communication

Create trust

Show respect and support for others

1. Communication

This is often cited as the most important of all relational skills, and it is as complex as it is important. Basically, good communication involves the sending and receiving of messages. It's not just about speaking to and hearing from people: it's about understanding the complete message.

It's useful to think of communication as an interdependent system, with four main components to consider. Firstly, the sender – this might be you, or anyone else. What do the words say? What is the motivation behind the words? What does the sender feel about the message? Does the sender have all the correct information? There is much more to understanding the message than simply hearing the words spoken.

Secondly, the listener is 'active' in the communication process as well. What is he or she expecting to hear? What assumptions will they bring to the process? How will they change what they think they will hear? How can both parties check that the message that has been sent has been correctly understood and interpreted?

Thirdly, the message itself. What format or media has been used to send the message? Is it the best one for that particular message? Is it an appropriate length? Does it have enough of the correct information needed to be fully understood?

Lastly, the 'context' of the communication is important. What is going on around the message? Is there high emotion? What are the consequences of it being misunderstood? What are the personal circumstances of both the listener and the sender?

Good communication minimises what is known as the 'arc of distortion', that is the gap between what the sender intends to communicate, and what the listener actually hears: this is critical for good relationships.

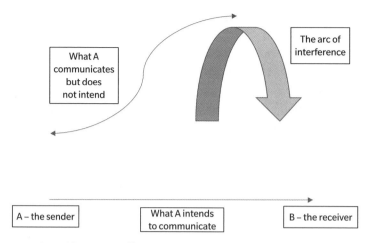

What A communicates but does not intend		The arc of interference

A – the sender	What A intends to communicate	B – the receiver

Source: Adapted from: https://www.projectsmart.co.uk/communications-management/the-arc-of-distortion.php

We can see that for communication to be effective, we need to consider much more than simply 'good listening'. Furthermore, when communicating virtually, the arc of interference can easily expand, as it is difficult to gather the contextual information that is necessary for messages to be correctly understood.

2. Create trust

We know how important trust is in any relationship and this is as important at work as it is at home. To be trusted or 'trustworthy' at work means to deliver what you say you will do, to consistently keep your word and to be conscientious about doing so. It means acting reliably, not unpredictably, and it means that others can have confidence in how you will respond in each situation. But there is more to trust than simply being dependable. To be really trusted by others, they must feel that you 'have their back'. That means that what you do must be believed to be in their interests, not just yours. We will talk much more about this later in the book, but the issue of trust is one of those contextual factors in communication that we mentioned in the section above. If there is no trust in a relationship, the arc of interference is much greater, and communication will be much less effective.

3. Show respect and support for others

Shared respect between people should underpin all working relationships, and this needs to be visible and explicit, not just assumed. Demonstrating respect and support is a key way of generating trust and showing that we value all those we work with. It's vital that we treat everybody equally and fairly, that we show encouragement and recognition for all contributions, that we share information and knowledge to help others and that we are honest in our dealings with them. It is a basic human right to be respected and, if we do not feel it, our energy is consumed with dealing with the perceived unfairness and hurt and we cannot give of our best to work.

To truly show respect and support for others we must, of course, get to know them, to understand their strengths, their goals, their concerns. To strengthen our relationships it's important to really get to know people, to build rapport with them and to share something of ourselves. Good relationships do not simply emerge, they require investment of time and energy on both sides. Not only does this create the foundation of an ongoing partnership, but it also creates a strong platform from which difficulties can be resolved.

These three things are the fundamentals of good relationships and in this book, we will look at how the new working reality requires us to make subtle changes to the way we use and develop these skills.

Whether you are in an office together, or on a Zoom or Microsoft Teams call with colleagues around the world, effective working relationships are the key to achieving your own objectives and those of your organisation. This claim is supported by research, particularly a classic study conducted in the 1990s by The Center for Creative Leadership in America. They followed the career paths of a group of young, high-potential managers destined for success and noted that, while some of the participants did indeed go on to achieve the career triumphs that had been predicted for them, others did not. Some of these others demonstrated a career 'plateau' achieving a certain level of seniority, but then progressing no further, while others seemed to fall backwards in their attainments. The research claimed that one of the most significant factors contributing to the failure of these people to realise their potential was 'An inability to develop and maintain effective working relationships'.

The rest of this book will help you to avoid such relational dangers.

chapter 2

Why are relationships so messy?

'Nothing is perfect. Life is messy. Relationships are complex. Outcomes are uncertain. People are irrational.'

Hugh Mackay, Australian reporter and author

As we have already established, relationships are a hugely complex area and can be very messy. In this respect, the relationships we develop with the people in our work life are no different to those we develop in our personal and social life. Each different type of relationship has the potential to be rewarding, easy, collaborative, challenging, frustrating, difficult, toxic and so on – in fact, complex and messy. In recent years the change from working in an office with all our workmates around us to a more blended way of working has added complications and different dimensions to how we manage and develop our working relationships. This change has led to additional possibilities for challenges and messiness in relationships.

In this chapter we will explore what contributes to this complexity and messiness in work-based relationships. We will look at how you can mitigate against too much messiness and will encourage you to reflect about your current work-based relationship network to review the quality of these relationships.

Why are relationships so complex and messy?

Relationships at work, whether they be with your boss/s, peers, direct reports, customers, suppliers or any other person, are complicated and ambiguous. One of the reasons for this is that we often have no choice about the people we have to work with and therefore whom we have to have some sort of relationship with. One of our bosses used to say, 'I don't ask you to like them or be their best friend, I just need you to work effectively together'. Typically, he said this when one of us had problems with someone we worked with. It was a useful reminder that we have little choice about our workmates and that we all have to find ways of interacting and working together.

So why might we find some relationships easier and more fulfilling than others and what makes some relationships become complicated, testing and possibly go off the rails? Before we explore this area, we suggest you reflect about and list the key people you currently have in your work-based relationship network. One of our preferred ways of doing this is to use a mind mapping process where you get a blank sheet of paper and put your name in the middle then annotate around it with the names and their relationship to you (boss, peer, colleague, customer, etc.).

We will come back to this mind map later, but for the moment it is sufficient to create the image with names and their relationship to you. By using a mind mapping technique, you are creating an image that can be added to and used for analysis and reflection purposes. Of course, if you prefer to simply make a list that's OK too.

Now back to the issue of what contributes to the complexity, ambiguity and potential messiness of these relationships and what might have an effect upon this. The chart below illustrates some of the things that we believe play a part in potential challenges in work-based relationships. Simply draw lines between you and the others you have working relationships with. Include their job titles if that helps.

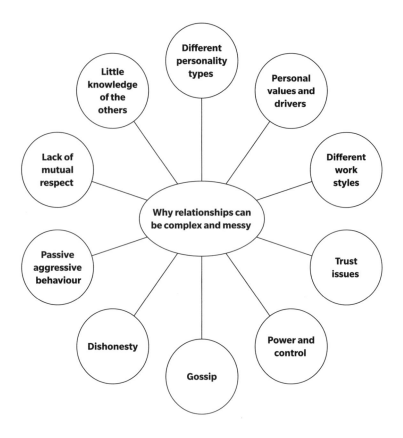

Let's look at each of these areas.

Different personality types

Categorising personality is an intricate process. There are countless different theories about this and no doubt many of you will have completed some of the myriad of personality questionnaires that tend to feature in both recruitment and development programmes. The most popular of which are the Myers Briggs Type Indicator®, the 16PF, the SHL Occupational Personality Questionnaire and the Hogan Personality Inventory (the 'Big 5' theory of personality). All of these questionnaires, and many of the others on the market today, seek to explain various traits and aspects of personality. When you complete the questionnaire the report that emerges will describe, using a range of parameters, what your likes and dislikes are and what your typical behaviour might be in certain situations and circumstances.

For instance, many of the questionnaires examine introversion and extroversion. Each one of these will have particular preferences for how we manage the relationships in our lives, and we will have both inclinations and disinclinations. An example of where relationships can become messy with the introversion/extroversion preference might be that in a team meeting comprising both introverts and extroverts, there could be misunderstandings between how **extroverts** work and communicate – chatty, think out aloud, speak quickly, generally enjoy thinking things through with others – and how **introverts** like to work and communicate – more introspective, like to think things through, prefer working alone and need time to re-energise after social interactions. After a meeting you may hear an extrovert say, 'That was a great meeting, we all had an opportunity to share our ideas' while an introvert might say 'I'm exhausted. Why do X and Y have to talk so much? What we really needed on this issue was time to think'.

Of course, this is only one aspect of personality – there are many others. The important issue is to observe and be aware of the personality differences between yourself and others and reflect about how you might adapt your behaviour in order to work towards effective outcomes with any person causing you challenges. Frequently, small adaptations in your normal behaviour pattern can make huge differences in challenging situations. For instance, you might be working with someone who tends to talk about the big picture, but you tend towards a highly detailed way of working and like to know as much as possible about an issue before committing to any action. In a situation like this you could try to modify your behaviour to accommodate the other person's needs in order to reach a mutually acceptable way forward, for instance by allowing the other person to describe their big picture perspective and you asking them questions about how this might work. Adapting behaviour in this way shows flexibility and a willingness to accommodate others' needs in service of a harmonious working environment.

Personal values and drivers

We all have different personal values and drivers that contribute to many of the decisions we make about our work. Values are those things that are important to us: the behaviours and characteristics that drive our motivations and decisions. Among other things, our values will influence the choices about the organisation we work for and the job we do. In addition, your values and drivers will also have an effect on how you relate to others.

Shared values will contribute to an effective relationship, whereas if you have to compromise your values it will often lead to difficulties. One's values tend to be driven by our deeply held beliefs, and if these are challenged or denied by someone then you may find it difficult to work together. For instance, honesty is regarded by many as a core value. If you work with someone and you discover that they have been dishonest with you about something, then this will erode the relationship, which will initially cause some changes and perhaps a bit of tension – another level of messiness. This sort of adjustment is typical of the micro changes that can lead to relationship tensions and ultimately breakdown.

If you are feeling that one of your work-based relationships is becoming challenging and difficult, you may like to ask yourself whether or not your personal values or drivers are being compromised in some way. Awareness of your values will help here. You might like to give some thought to your own personal values and drivers at work. List the top five or ten values that you hold dear and are your guiding principles for the way you like to work. Typical examples of these might be – honesty, trust, dependability, integrity, positive attitude and adaptability. Once you know what your values are and how they contribute to your day-to-day work and relationships you will have a greater understanding of why you react badly when they are challenged or denied.

My personal values	Guiding principles

Different work styles

We all have different styles of working. One model for looking at work styles is described in the chart below:

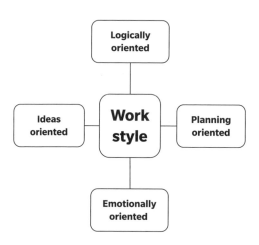

Work style	Typical features	Benefits
Logically oriented	Rational, judicious, methodical, with a preference for facts and data	Demonstrates knowledge. Clarity in thinking. Makes decisions. Action oriented.
Planning oriented	Structured, meticulous, detail focussed, systematic	Well prepared and thought through. Clear in setting out expectations.
Emotionally oriented	Cooperative, collaborative, appreciative, empathetic	Involves others. Builds on others' ideas. Gets buy-in from colleagues.
Ideas oriented	Energetic, expressive, creative, eloquent, enjoys brainstorming	Effective in times of change. Involves and inspires lots of people.

Each of these work styles has different features and behaviours and can be affected by, for instance, our personality, our values, the culture of the organisation, our level of experience, our level of confidence and so on. They are often the source of emotional turmoil and can lead to disagreements and confrontation between people. Different work styles are common between work colleagues. Successful teams and organisations are made up of diverse groups of people who all bring different skills, styles, abilities and competence to the demands of their jobs. When people of differing styles have to work together, they often experience opinion and process inconsistencies which can lead to disagreements and relationship breakdowns.

You might like to think about which one of these styles would be most descriptive of your work style. You could also refer back to your list or mind map image of the people in your work-based relationship group and try to categorise each person's work style. This might also help you to make sense of some of these relationships and why some are easy and rewarding and others are more challenging.

Trust issues

One of the most important elements of any good-quality relationship is mutual trust. Without trust the social glue that contributes to effective work-based relationships is eroded. Trust is developed between people based on a variety of elements – reliability, capability, consideration and communication – all of which have to work together for success and so that you can truly feel that mutual trust exists and can consequently depend and rely on these other people.

You might like to think about and identify one or two people that you regard as trustworthy work colleagues. Once you have identified them, you should give some thought as to why this is the case. This will help you to understand more about what creates trust between people. It might also be useful to think about a person you feel you cannot trust and reflect why this is the case and what the impact of this lack of trust has on your relationship.

We will explore more about trust later in this book in Chapter 6.

Power and control

Some degree of power exists in most relationships, which helps you to have a feeling of being in control. Being in control leads to feelings of empowerment, which in turn helps you to do such things as manage yourself, your relationships with others, your emotions, how you influence and how you make decisions. Problems arise when the power relationship becomes imbalanced and one person tries to exert unfair levels of power and control over another. Think about a time when this imbalance has happened between you and a colleague. What did the other person do or say that made you feel that the power/control balance had become imbalanced?

Gossip

Probably one of the most common reasons for 'messy' relationship issues is the prevalence of gossip in your organisation's culture. The definition of gossip is idle talk or rumour, often about the private affairs of others. Most of us will gossip at work to some degree or another. While all gossip can be detrimental, the most dangerous type is when you are being malicious or critical about a person behind their back. The best way of ensuring this does not contribute to messiness in your relationships is to avoid gossiping about other people.

Dishonesty

This is simply unacceptable and will always lead to relationship breakdown. People can be dishonest for all sorts of reasons, but you can often find that the deceitful person uses various tactics to get ahead in the organisation and promote themselves. Typical examples of the sort of deceptions might be:

- misleading people about their role in the organisation, perhaps by not being totally honest about job title or who they report to
- taking credit for work done by or with others; for instance, when a person suggests that they authored a report or pitched a brilliant idea without crediting the others involved, thus stealing all the glory.

Dishonesty can be pervasive, leading to a toxic culture and increased staff turnover where people find it difficult to trust one another or to have meaningful and productive relationships.

Passive aggressive behaviour

This type of behaviour is complicated and confusing. The sort of behaviour you may experience from someone who is passive aggressive includes:

- sarcasm
- eye rolling when in group interactions
- blaming others
- backhanded compliments
- saying 'yes' but meaning 'no'
- making excuses.

The confusion comes because people who use passive aggressive behaviour are often feeling angry, resentful, frustrated but have the ability to act in a natural or even pleasant and cheerful manner. This type of behaviour, invariably, subtly undermines anyone involved.

This type of behaviour can lead to significant messiness, misunderstanding and bad feeling between people. One way of dealing with such behaviour is firstly to recognise that it is happening so looking out for the clues and then reacting by calling the person out by asking them a question; for instance, by asking them to 'say a bit more about what they are feeling'.

Lack of mutual respect

Building and developing mutual respect at work helps to build healthy workplaces with good-quality relationships and reduces stress and conflict. Typically, mutual respect is gained by demonstrating good communication techniques both verbal and non-verbal, being courteous, taking time to get to know the people you work with and keeping control of negative emotional displays.

Lack of mutual respect between work colleagues may be demonstrated by such behaviours as:

- interrupting
- using belittling comments in meetings
- joking at someone else's expense
- excluding people from group meetings.

When this sort of behaviour happens, relationships quickly break down and harmony and effectiveness between people disappears.

Little knowledge of the others

Getting to know the people you work with is important for success in relationships. This is an issue that can be challenging for a variety of reasons:

- when people work from home for much of the time

- some people simply do not want to let people at work get too close
- some personality types can be challenging to get to know
- the time and space available for social interaction in your organisation.

The depth of your knowledge of others of course will vary and much will depend upon the individual themselves and how much and what they wish to share with workmates. The important issue in this area is that people have the opportunity to get to know each other at a social as well as a work-based level. Organisational culture plays a major role in this area if there is a general commitment towards people being encouraged to work together while also having time and space to have social time. For instance: organisations can provide space for people to meet informally for coffee/lunch/ informal get-togethers and organisational leaders and managers can build time into their meetings for some social interaction as well as focussing on the business element.

Tips for keeping relationships healthy

- Keep an open mind about people whether you like them or not.
- Recognise that difference is good. When you realise that one of the reasons you might be finding a relationship tricky is due to your different personality types, give some thought to these differences and identify the positives that might develop from accommodating the other person's preferences. This does not mean you are changing your personality, you are simply flexing your behaviour during an interaction to help maintain a positive relationship.
- Find opportunities to share your values with other people and explore together what they mean to you and why they are important. When people have a greater understanding of each other's values they are more likely to respect them.

- Different work styles are a fact of organisational life and contribute to diversity in the workplace. When you identify that work style is contributing to a 'messy' relationship, first of all identify what you think the other person's work style might be and which particular behavioural traits are causing problems. Then, thinking about your own preferences in work style and the behaviours you would tend to use on a day-to-day basis, give some thought to how you might adapt and flex your own behaviour to enable you to work together for the short term.

- When you realise that gossip is an issue in your work environment make sure you do not participate, never pass gossip on, turn the gossip round by offering a positive perspective on the person, and finally you could confront the person spreading the gossip by calling them out. Once someone is challenged about gossiping and knows that they have been caught out, they are far less likely to continue in the future.

- Pay attention and allocate time to thinking about your work relationships.

chapter 3

—

Relationship agility: low key or high value?

'Success today requires the agility and drive to constantly rethink, reinvigorate, react, and reinvent.'

Bill Gates, co-founder of Microsoft and The Bill & Melinda Gates Foundation

The good news is that whether you work in one of the largest companies – such as Amazon with over a million staff worldwide – or in one of the smallest, the skills and abilities you need for relationship agility are similar. Later in this chapter we will look at different ways to develop a few of these skills. But let's first take a look more broadly at how communication is different in this digital age.

What's different about communication in the digital age

Undoubtedly, this digital age with all its technology options has made life easier in many respects and few of us would wish to go back to a pre-digital time even if it were possible. However, in the modern workplace certain aspects are different, and these have an impact on relationships – on how we communicate and connect with each other. Two of the most obvious changes to the business world that have a major impact on our relationships at work are the increasing amount of information that we now deal with, and the speed with which we exchange information and communicate with one another.

The increasing speed of communication

The accelerated speed of communication and rapid information transfer has increased phenomenally across all businesses. Indeed, online trading in company stocks and shares happens in nanoseconds (high-frequency trading) and minutes can be vital in some sectors. One private airline company visited by two of the authors (Fiona and Viki) operates on tight deadlines to win business and also when resolving any problems. For instance, securing the chance to pitch for a new piece of work, 'being agile', may sometimes be down to a matter of minutes and having a lightning-speed response to beat fierce competition.

The implications of such response speed can undoubtedly be exhilarating: working at such a fast pace can be exciting. Less positive, however, is if this frenetic pace is relentless, as this will invariably create pressure. At first this might be manageable, but too long, or too much, will wear you down. It also has a domino effect, crowding out other key aspects of your role. One common casualty we often hear about is the thinking space and time for reflection, but this is not optional for anyone. It is vital to find time to pause for breath and to take stock. Otherwise, the danger is that you get lost in all the detail, don't improve how you work currently and don't plan ahead.

One CEO of a rapidly expanding meat company steps back from a fast-growing business every quarter to review future developments. Another person at board level jealously guards 'thinking time' in the diary explaining, 'it's crucial to help me focus on future issues for our division'.

Finding time to 'switch off' from all those daily distractions or that background noise going on around you is a valuable exercise whatever level of the business you are involved with. 'Chill time' also helps us to de-stress, something that everybody should consciously dial into their work regime. It has unfortunately become all too common these days to hear people talk about burnout and high levels of stress which are sometimes caused, and certainly compounded, by increased speed of information and overload. Michael Drayton's book *Anti-burnout*, as well as the TED Talk by psychologist Adam Grant, both contain useful advice and insight on this topic.

Information overload

The quantity of information available to all of us in business has grown exponentially over the past few years including a plethora of social media options as well as more traditional sources such as emails. Not only can we quickly and instantly send information to colleagues around us, but at the same time we can share this with a much wider group. But if everyone (rather than a few) decides to respond to the person sending that message, a sudden rush of replies might create overload. Of course, this is a single instance. Everyone who is involved in multiple projects is likely to face far more problems of overload today.

Dealing effectively with too much information, responding in a way that is both timely and efficient, is important. There is little point in responding too quickly to someone with the wrong information. Alternatively, sending out FYI (For Your Information) messages to too many is also not helpful. Of course, it can be tempting to keep everyone in the information loop, but always consider first if it is helping you to build and maintain effective relationships. This especially applies to those blanket messages deliberately sent out on a Friday afternoon in the hope they will soon be lost and overwhelmed by Monday's messages.

The scale of the problems experienced is illustrated by a person who returned from holiday to find 900 email messages. One response might be to spend the first day working through everything, although it might take longer than one day! What would you do then?

In this case he decided to ignore all of them saying, 'if anything is important then they will contact me again'. It did in fact work out as people did get in touch again with new messages, but it could also have gone horribly wrong.

What you can do to stop overload

There are various coping strategies for holiday problems. Some people check in every day to read through messages – a read-only strategy to stay ahead of developments back at work. Others prefer taking short breaks of a few days rather than a long time away.

Most effective teams we know establish 'housekeeping' rules: a protocol or coordinated approach focussed on practical strategies. Often these come under the heading of working smarter, rather than working harder. One team, for example, appoint a 'duty manager' so while messages from a range of clients arrive addressed to many team members, only one person deals with it. Everyone else can simply skim-read the different email or messaging threads in order to stay up to date.

Another team focus on a 'once-only' approach to read and immediately deal with each message, creating an environment that is action oriented. It did take quite a lot of practice to achieve this 'ideal', but it was definitely worthwhile as it made a significant improvement to the team's effectiveness. Is this a policy you could use, either for yourself or for teams you work with?

Think about ways to help stem the tide of information. Some companies, for example, have an 'Email-free Friday' and you could consider creating something similar with colleagues or customers. It's also worth considering how many messages you receive that are 'surplus', unnecessary pieces of information that clutter up your in-box. Are there ways you can improve how you deal with them, for example skim-reading the first few lines or, if these occur regularly, then sharing these between others in your team? Do not multitask, as flitting between different messages and across different projects saps your efficiency level, whereas staying focussed for significant amounts of time will help you to achieve more.

But let's now consider a few key skills to help you to build agility and maintain relationships in the digital age. It goes without saying that technical skills are important – making sure that you stay up to date and tech-savvy. As one HR Director said 'these days a good deal of the expertise among my team of thirty people is far more technically advanced than I am, but they all know that when I need to drill down into the detail then I will and can do this. I know the questions to ask and what the data will show us'. 'Otherwise' he says, 'my team would lose respect for me'.

Developing your relationship skills

We have identified four key components of communications to help improve your relationship agility as shown in the following figure. All of these represent a valuable skillset for face-to-face meetings but become especially useful when your connection is virtual. Rahul Guha of Boston Consulting Group in India recently said this means working 'twice as hard to get the same level of engagement' (Hill and Jacobs, 2021).

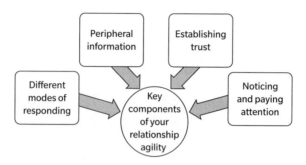

Four key components of relationship agility

Let's begin with different modes of responding.

Different modes of responding

People differ in how they absorb communication. Just think about how the introverts you work alongside respond in comparison to extraverts. Some people (often introverts) are more comfortable and creative with time for reflection. You need to accommodate these differences and make room for everyone to contribute fully.

Another difference is that some people prefer a short, high-level review of a topic while someone else will be more comfortable with a detailed report. Not just headline findings but a deep dive into the 'nuts and bolts' of it all. Not to mention the spontaneous colleague who enjoys a more relaxed attitude to planning compared to others around them who prefer to plan and find spontaneity difficult to deal with. Establishing, surfacing and understanding these preferences in any relationship is important and will pay dividends in terms of building rapport and a strong team. When you find a relationship is becoming messy and not going well it is often these issues that are creating tension.

Another aspect of responding concerns attitudes and behaviours. Eric Berne, who worked as a psychiatrist in the 1950s and 1960s, observed three different states of mind, of ego – parent, adult and child – which change how we respond to one another. As a theory of transactional analysis his model became popular in the following decades and applied in various settings.

If you are not familiar with this, then a simple example is that a good work relationship would be 'adult–adult': where both sides are professional, take responsibility and behave in a grown-up way acting with integrity and empathy. If instead the relationship switches to become 'parent–child', then the parent might deliver a lecture about whatever is being discussed. You may see examples of this both at work and at home as it's very easy to slip into such roles and we sometimes do this unconsciously.

One of Eric Berne's best-selling books *Games People Play* is still available, and the title exactly captures those elements of bad behaviour and ego issues. A typical example is where some members of a group decide to 'opt out' of decision-making. It can take a while to realise what is going wrong but, in the meantime, it can be very disruptive to the rest of the group. Perhaps you can recall other examples in your current job or from a previous role. Your first task is to understand why it is happening and then to take action to resolve whatever the key issue is about. Focus always on how behaviours should change and what you want to see as an outcome.

Peripheral information

Peripheral information is not only thinking about whether a room is too hot or too cold to create a good meeting space, and whether lunch has been ordered, it is also about appreciating the non-verbal cues that are always available to us. Body language and non-verbal behaviours these days are both familiar phrases and can be your early-warning signal when a meeting or conversation is going off track. For instance, if everyone involved is paying close attention to the person speaking then this is a good sign. A bad sign, a lack of respect, would be if one or two people involved in the conversation start swiping down their phone screens, respond to every 'ping' message sound or are completely disengaged staring out the window.

Another negative red flag is someone impatiently watching the time conveying the message of either 'I am bored' or 'I am too important to waste my time here'. Alexandra Shulman, editor of *Vogue* magazine until 2017, describes an incident in mid-conversation when the person she was talking to lost interest, 'they had stopped listening' (Shulman, 2016). Picking up quickly on these signs and being able to reconnect is a valuable skill. As described, this might sound an obvious change, but it is surprisingly common to find people who do not see such signals.

Your own non-verbal behaviours, and those around you, should create focus (on the topic and people concerned), interest and energy. One of the most obvious ways to engage is to use open body language and eye contact, to nod when there is agreement and smile at the other person. A smile can light up your face and immediately creates rapport with another person. Conversely, if you start the meeting with closed body language (arms crossed in a defensive manner) and avoid eye contact or smiling, then the message is completely altered.

Working in multinationals can help you understand the differences between various nationalities, generations and cultures more quickly. A key issue is to proceed with caution when you are in a new environment rather than making assumptions that everywhere will be the same. Your facial expressions, mannerisms, quick signals such as a 'thumbs up', as well as the personal distance you leave between you and the other person (known as proxemics) may all differ. All can make a difference. Back in the 1960s, psychologist Paul Ekman's research identified six universal expressions or emotions namely: fear, anger, sadness, happiness, disgust and surprise (Ekman, 2004). Facial expressions are a key part of building rapport, to build awareness of your own behaviours and consider the impact this has on others. In addition, consider the physical distance between people in a group or who is standing up and who is allowed to sit down.

Who is fidgeting? You can learn a good deal from observing those around you. We all do it, either consciously or unconsciously, so look for examples and notice when the message and the body language are aligned, and when they do not align.

Establishing trust

Finding ways to build trust with other people is a crucial component of any relationship – whether that's in our personal life or at work. We often talk about 'can I trust him or her?' And when a work relationship turns sour or takes a massive dive downwards, people will often say, 'what can I do to rebuild the level of trust we once had?'

Trust and respect can quickly be lost if one side behaves in a way that is unacceptable to the other. For example, when someone does not deliver as agreed or if they deliberately tell a lie, this can cause resentment: a feeling of being let down or, alternatively, not being treated with respect. Rebuilding such a damaged relationship can be hard. However, you might like to consider the difference between how you are prepared to 'forgive and forget' with young children compared to how sometimes we will be unforgiving and bear a grudge at work. If the relationship is to function well going forward, you must be prepared to find common ground again.

Trust, once established, can be long-lasting; for instance, when in the role of Chancellor of the Exchequer, British Prime Minister Rishi Sunak talked about this as he is still in touch with those who mentored him early on in his career (Tyler, 2022). We know of many other early friendships at work that have continued over the years. Trust is all about being open and honest, authentic and genuine. How often do people around you praise you for any of these qualities? If you want to improve work relationships, you must understand the vital role of trust. Chapter 6 looks in more detail at trust.

Noticing and paying attention

What we mean by noticing and paying attention is your ability to tune into a variety of different sources. One illustration of this is if some colleagues on a call are gradually contributing less and less, would you notice if it happens in meetings you are involved with? Some people talk about those who use their antenna well. Ask yourself, how good are your observation and listening skills? Do you give people your undivided attention or are you an inveterate multitasker? Do you pay sufficient attention to the world around you or are you always self-centred with head down and task focussed? For instance, think about the three questions below.

Noticing and paying attention

One: Would you notice if a colleague is constantly tired and unexpectedly making mistakes or does someone have to point this out to you?

Two: Do you notice when body language has switched into a negative mode; for example, is someone suddenly frowning, looking vacant, starting to fidget or sitting with arms folded in a defensive way? What is not being said?

Three: Do you understand the relevance of subtle messages or comments made to you? For example, perhaps your boss has told you a few times that you are too aggressive or, alternatively, too passive in meetings.

Let's take each of these in turn. If perhaps you would not pick up on those signals from your tired colleague in question one, then you would not be alone as this, unfortunately, frequently happens – though it should not. Being self-absorbed creates significant dangers for you. Not paying attention or reading the subtle clues from those around you means you lose a valuable source of feedback.

The second point highlights the value of paying close attention to what body language can tell you. Often this happens before the conversation takes too much of a negative turn and so provides an early warning system for you to pick up on. It's particularly valuable in some meetings to allocate this role to someone to watch out for such issues. As noted earlier, a smile in America is a positive sign but as Steve Rosenberg, the BBC's Russia correspondent, recently highlighted someone who smiles too much in Russia is likely to be thought foolish, which is why President Vladimir Putin is so often seen with a stern face and so rarely smiles (in broadcast on BBC Radio 4, 2021).

The third point is that some comments or messages, either subtle or not so subtle, can reveal flaws either in your approach or your attitude, which you should have listened to. One example, a typical story often heard in career coaching sessions is, 'my boss did mention a few times that I was too aggressive, took "no prisoners", etc., but I didn't realise it would be the key barrier to my next promotion'. Maybe the first time the comment was said you thought it was a joke and so you did not take it to heart.

How to manage these skills in online meetings

Do you notice body language in meetings? Are you aware of the impact of your own body language or those around you? A good way to check this is to ask someone impartial to give you feedback after a meeting, ask them to provide specific examples or take a video recording so you can both look through this together. Then observe other people in meetings and look for times when non-verbal behaviours are aligned or out of alignment with what is being said.

The more you practise this skill, the better you will become. Nick Morgan's book on virtual communications talks about how a virtual world strips out emotional content from our messages. One tip to improve your body language in virtual meetings offered by entrepreneur Bianca Miller Coles, is to avoid touching your hair and face too often as this will make you seem nervous or inattentive. In her book *Digital Body Language*, Erica Dhawan highlights the dangers of speeding up – as everyone expects conversations online to be continuous without the natural pauses we use face to face: 'slow down to speed up'. It's great advice.

chapter 4

Why relationship awareness matters

'The easiest kind of relationship for me is with 10,000 people. The hardest is with one!'

Joan Baez, singer, songwriter, musician and activist

Relationship awareness is about understanding the intricacies of relationship development and management within organisational life. People and organisations are both complex and complicated, and we have to develop the ability to work well with others to ensure effectiveness and success in our working lives. The Center for Creative Leadership (CCL) have identified poor working relations as one of the top five reasons why people 'derail' in their career. CCL, who have been studying derailment since 1983, found clear evidence that relationship challenges can lead to people not achieving their full potential and for some resulted in a seemingly promising career going off track – derailment. This, as well as our own experience of the stories we hear about relationship challenges and issues at work from many leaders, managers and executives, makes relationship awareness one of the key areas to focus on for working effectively with others.

In these days of increased hybrid working where people are not wholly office based, relationships with colleagues often have to be developed and built via Zoom, Microsoft Teams and similar video conferencing technology. During the Covid-19 pandemic in 2020/21 many people never met their colleagues face to face, and those starting new roles even had their onboarding all done online. While many of the same rules apply, this new way of working presents more challenges for relationship awareness and development.

In this chapter we will explore and examine in more depth what motivates people to develop relationships at work, why people develop and sustain these relationships and what makes them successful or unsuccessful. We will also introduce you to a model to help you to categorise, develop and understand your relationships in a more holistic way. In addition to this we will also explore how to get the best out of your relationships when you do not have the opportunity to meet face to face on a regular basis, and we will look at some of the pitfalls and challenges of relationship development in hybrid working.

What is relationship awareness?

Essentially, relationship awareness is about understanding the basis of our relationships with others. By recognising where we are in our relationships, we can explore why we create and develop them and determine what we need to do to improve, develop or adjust them appropriately. Any type of relationship is complex and intricate with all sorts of ups and downs along the way whether the relationship is work based, social or family. In all our relationships we experience both good times when a relationship is positive and supportive and bad times when it is challenging and difficult. The starting point for us is understanding why we are in any relationship. We believe that this makes it easier to work out which relationships are most valuable and require investment and development and which are less valuable. This does not mean that the less valuable relationships should be dropped but rather it will prompt you to re-evaluate them. Part of the re-evaluation may involve identifying the relationships you could drop or at least spend less time on. It is often the case that without this kind of review you never realise that you are spending too much time on dysfunctional relationships such as those with a team member who is increasingly taking up too much of your energy and time. If you allow this to happen it can have ramifications for your other colleagues who are doing good work but feel you are not spending as much time with them.

Developing and maintaining good-quality relationships is a huge investment, taking much time and effort. For your self-worth, self-confidence and self-awareness, it is important that you understand and recognise the purpose of each relationship. Knowing why you have a relationship with a person will help you get the most from it.

What motivates people to develop relationships with others?

Based on research which was done by Fiona at Ashridge Business School where she surveyed and interviewed thousands of business managers and executives, we identified a range of reasons why people develop and build relationships at work. The same research also identified what tended to contribute towards good-quality and rewarding relationships and what made relationships go toxic.

The chart that follows summarises the responses to the survey in these important areas:

What makes people develop and build relationships at work?

• Fun and social banter	• To provide new opportunities
• Having something in common	• To provide a listening ear
• To get work done	• Because I like people
• Shared sense of humour	• Shared interests
• Participation in joint projects	• Common goals
• General liking of people	• I have regular contact with them
• Sharing knowledge and experience	• Enjoy working with others
	• To keep people happy
• To promote my career	• The boss told me to

From this research we identified that there are three clear reasons as to why people created relationships:

• because they work in the same team or department

• because you believe they can help you perform your role and achieve your goals

• because you like the person and want to develop a more friendly relationship with them.

When we began to delve deeper into this area it became clear that the quality and depth of a person's relationships at work depended to a large extent upon their emotional connection with others. This connection could either be at a personal level where you enjoy each other's company, or it can be more transactional and related to needing each other to get the job done. This led us to develop a model to help people analyse, assess and understand the relationships they develop at work.

Before we introduce you to the model you might like to categorise your work-based relationships onto the chart below where we use three levels of relationship:

- Acquaintances – the people you know at work, who may be friendly enough and who you speak to in terms of day-to-day pleasantries, but they are not central to your success in your role.

- Mates, friends and colleagues – the people you spend time with each day where your involvement is more in depth and they have some degree of impact on your effectiveness and success in your job.

- Inner circle – those extremely close work colleagues on whom you depend both on a work and on an emotional level. These are the people who have a direct impact on your success in your job.

Use the chart below or copy it onto a sheet of paper and categorise and note down the people in your work-based relationships:

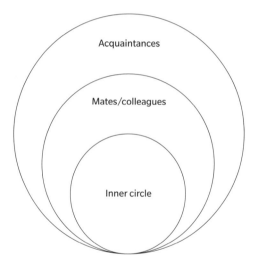

This exercise will encourage you to reflect about and identify all the people you have relationships with at work. As we have said before, this can be quite complex and intricate with people from all over the organisation as well as people outside the company like clients, suppliers, consultants and so on. This should then help you when you move on to attempt to categorise these relationships into the relationship awareness model, which is illustrated and explained below.

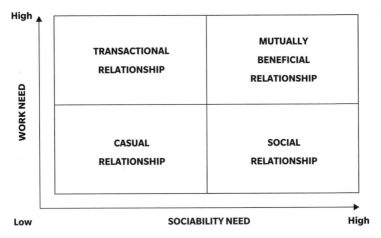

Relationship awareness model

Source: Dent, F. (2009) *The Working Relationships Pocketbook.* Management Pocketbooks

Let's look at the features of each of these four types of relationship.

- **Casual relationship** – this type of relationship has both low work and low social need and is typically not an essential relationship and often of a superficial nature. An example of a casual relationship might be people who you see on an occasional basis or who are part of your day-to-day contacts. For example, the security people or receptionists at your workplace: people you chat to and pass the time of day with but probably know little about.

- **Social relationship** – where there is a low work need but high social need often typified by an emotional connection that has led to friendship. There is little need in relation to your day-to-day work, but you enjoy each other's company and have a good level of mutual trust. This is a person whom you actually choose to spend time with, and you may on occasions use them as a sounding board for ideas.

- **Transactional relationship** – people who fall into this category are those with whom you have a high work need but low social need: someone who you have a professional relationship with in order to get your job done but share little in common other than that. For instance, a colleague from another team who you have to work with in order to win a piece of business but who you would not normally choose to spend time with. These relationships can be challenging and tricky as they largely depend upon some level of '*quid pro quo*' or mutual exchange between the parties involved where they make an agreement to support one another in service of the goal and outcome. If this need was not there, then this would be a person very much on the periphery of your relationship network, probably falling in the casual relationship category.

- **Mutually beneficial relationship** – these people are front and centre of your relationship network. For you there is a high work need and a high social need where the relationship has a dual purpose: it serves both as a friendship and also helps to get your job done. These people will be the ones you enjoy being with: you have a good level of respect for them and you probably know them well. It is likely to be a relationship that has been developed over time based on the experience you have had when sharing and discussing ideas, knowledge and developing projects together. They generally help you to work things out and move forward with your goals and objectives.

It's now time to categorise the major relationships in your day-to-day working life. Use the information from the chart you created earlier. On the chart and beside each person's name think about each one and consider the level of work and social need that applies to them. Now position each person onto the chart in the place that represents your current thoughts about the quality of the relationship. You are likely to have people in some or all of the quadrants.

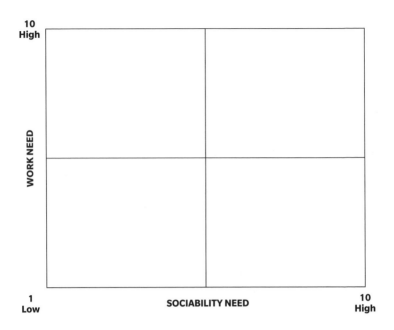

Once you have completed your chart you should ask yourself:

- How you feel about the scatter of the relationships – is this a true reflection?

- Do you feel that you should be attempting to move any of the relationships from one box to another? For instance, you may think that a person who is currently located in the 'social relationship' quadrant could, with a little time and effort, be nudged up into the 'mutually beneficial' quadrant and would therefore become a more effective relationship. How might you do this?

- Are there any people who you have put onto your chart that you currently invest too much time and effort in? How might you adapt such a relationship without compromising on the quality of it?

- Looking at the chart now are there any people who you think should be added and in whom you should invest time to develop that relationship?

What does the overall pattern of your relationships tell you about your attitude to relationships at work?

It's important to note that not all relationships should fall into the mutually beneficial quadrant. It is quite acceptable to have people in all four quadrants. The important issue is to recognise where they are, what the impact of this is for the quality of the relationship and whether or not you could further develop the relationships for greater effectiveness.

For instance, recognising that someone falls into the 'transactional quadrant' means that this person is necessary for you to get your job done but it is not someone you would tend to confide in or spend much 'social' time with. This is fine but you must recognise it and ensure you adapt and flex your behaviour accordingly by thinking about the person's personality, preferred way of communicating and adopting the appropriate influencing approach (see Chapter 9).

Analysing your relationship networks in this way will help you to determine whether or not you have the necessary people in your network, who you might wish to add to it, which relationships you want to invest more in and how you can develop each relationship to be more effective.

This type of analysis can be helpful whether you work largely face to face or online.

What makes relationships successful or unsuccessful?

In our research we also asked people 'What in your view makes work-based relationships successful and rewarding?' and 'What makes relationships go wrong?' Many reasons were offered but we have categorised the features for successful relationships into these four areas:

- a common bond
- personal interest
- openness
- honesty.

Some of the things people said were – we have shared goals; they listen to me; we 'clicked' from the start; we have fun; we share a sense of humour; there was a mutual respect between us; they had a real energy about them.

The reasons identified for relationships turning toxic are:

- being let down
- misunderstanding.

What people said was – they were arrogant; they seemed pushy; we didn't have a connection; they took me for granted; they had a bad attitude; conversation was always one way.

Successful relationships are built on many things but what we do know is that time, energy and commitment are necessary. Being relationally aware will contribute to the success of all your work-based relationships whether face to face or virtual. How would you describe the reasons that your relationships are successful or not?

Hybrid working and relationship development

Working virtually does not come easily to us all – seeing your colleagues on a computer screen is a very different way of managing our relationships at work. Even before many of us were forced into virtual working by the Covid-19 pandemic it was clear that hybrid working had become more popular. What the pandemic did was make it even more likely to be a regular feature of working life of the future. So how can you ensure that you make the most of your relationships virtually?

There are no easy ways of replacing face-to-face relationships. However, focussing on the development of a range of areas that contribute to your skill and authenticity when working virtually in this new hybrid world of work will contribute to how you manage your relationships at work. Some practical areas to focus on are:

Self-presentation → Individual interaction → Be fully present

- How you present yourself. Think about the impact you want to have on other people when you are communicating online. Some of the things to focus on:

  ○ Body language – think about how you use your facial expressions, hand and arm gestures and posture to convey warmth and interest during your online conversations. Smiling, maintaining a fluidity of movement and a generally relaxed and welcoming posture will all help. Use nods and other appropriate movements to show you are engaged with the other person/people.

  ○ Vocal usage – think about how you use your voice to convey your feelings and enthusism. Vary your pace, pitch and volume to maintain interest, variety and energy. Try to avoid vocal tics such as um, ar, mmm . . . all of which can detract from the quality of the conversation.

- How you interact with people individually, when online, is key to the development of positive, quality relationships. As with face to face, eye contact is vital for developing trust and authenticity. Online this can be quite challenging as it involves looking at the camera rather than the screen. The temptation for most of us when communicating online is to look at the screen, but if you do this and your camera is at the top of your computer screen then it will appear as if you are looking down. To ensure your eye contact appears as natural as possible, look at the camera as you would look someone in the eyes in a face-to-face conversation; that is, don't stare but look for several seconds at a time. To help make this easier ensure your webcam is at eye level. Another way of making your interactions more personal is to ensure you use inclusive language – we, our – and the present tense. Also be careful to avoid interrupting others as this is a sign of lack of interest and poor manners.

- Being fully present during your meetings is vital. A comfortable chair, appropriate workspace with good lighting and fresh air will all contribute to maintaining presence. Especially in one-to-one meetings don't switch off your camera or microphone as this can appear to others that you are distracted and not fully present. Practise active listening skills by asking follow-on questions, testing understanding and using a summary and checking understanding. These skills demonstrate focus and interest in what's going on at the meeting as well as in the people taking part. Give everyone involved space to talk and contribute by speaking less and listening more. Use questions to bring others in – especially those who are less vocal. In both face-to-face and virtual conversations, people underestimate the power and value of a well-thought-through and timed question.

These practical areas of thinking about presence, interacting with others by such things as maintaining eye contact, avoiding interrupting each other, ensuring others are listening, dealing with questions fairly and ensuring everyone has a hearing are all very important for successful virtual working and for relationship awareness, development and thinking about your virtual image and character.

Features of dysfunctional relationships

It is also important to recognise when a relationship is becoming or has become dysfunctional. Some of the key features to be aware of that indicate dysfunctionality include:

- communication becoming one sided and counterproductive
- constant criticism and demeaning comments are a regular occurrence
- a growing feeling of discomfort when interacting with the person
- feelings of dislike between people
- conflict is a permanent feature of a relationship
- different ways of doing things leading to unproductive competitive behaviour.

When a relationship has become dysfunctional you don't have to give up on it. In fact, it can be the case that if you are able to work things out then the relationship can be more positive and stronger than ever. There are a couple of things you should do. First and most importantly recognise that it is dysfunctional, and secondly review what has gone wrong and why. This can often point you in the direction of the way ahead and will help you to plan how you can adapt your behaviour in order to determine whether or not you are able to salvage the relationship. However, there are no quick fixes: it takes time, energy and effort to get a relationship back on track and often it leads to a new improved way of working together.

Remember respect and honesty with yourself and others is a major part of creating, developing and maintaining healthy relationships in all walks of life.

chapter 5

How resilient are you?

'Do not judge me by my success, judge me by how many times I fell down and got back up again.'

Anonymous

Resilience is popularly regarded as the ability to bounce back from any adversities, failures, tough times and difficulties posed by life events. Hasson and Hadfield in their book *Bounce* say resilience is 'the ability to bounce back after misfortune'. How we respond to day-to-day misfortunes such as relationship breakdowns, illness, job loss, or indeed world-changing events like the recent pandemic, war or a natural disaster such as floods and how we move on from them is largely down to our personality, value system, personal coping strategies and attitudes to life in general. Individuals vary a lot with regard to how they deal with failure, setbacks and difficulty. Like so many behavioural issues, how we react and ultimately cope will vary from person to person and situation to situation. Indeed, some people will relish the challenge of many of the testing situations life throws at us and even see them as opportunities while others will sink into the depths of despair and even depression and of course many other responses in between those two.

It is also important to make it clear that in this book we are primarily concerned with resilience in the context of our work life. The circumstances that any of us find ourselves in will obviously contribute to our resilience. For example, our response to dealing with a short-term setback such as losing a client might be completely different to how we deal with a longer-term or life-changing setback such as loss of a loved one or significant change in one's health. Certain personal characteristics (see below) will contribute no matter what, but if the setback is life changing in some way, we may need additional resources to draw upon.

This book is about working with others so is largely concerned with how we develop, build and maintain our relationships at work. In this chapter we will explore some general aspects about what resilience is and what your personal approach to resilience is. More specifically, we will focus on approaches for becoming more resilient regarding relationships and working with others and how you can get better at being resilient and helping others to develop their resilience. We will also reflect about the importance of the organisation's role in the resilience of its employees.

Resilience – what is it?

In *Harvard Business Review on Building Personal and Organisational Resilience*, Diane L. Coutu suggests that 'there are 3 characteristics that set resilient people and organisations apart'. These are:

- the capacity to accept and face down reality
- an ability to find meaning in some aspects of life
- the ability to improvise.

In addition to these points, we believe resilience is largely an attitude or state of mind, some of which is part of your personal DNA, personality and battery of strengths, some is related to how you have developed throughout your life and the experiences life has thrown at you.

For instance, during a recent coaching session with a senior manager who works for a large international bank we talked about the importance of resilience in relation to his and his colleague's performance at work. He firmly believes that lessons learned early in his life contribute to his current ability in the area of resilience. He talked about his time as a rugby player and the lessons he learned from that time in relation to early failures on the pitch, healthy eating, sleeping and balance in life and how that has continued into his corporate career and has helped him to maintain a level of resilience to this day. Stories like these are common, with many people who we have coached and trained telling us about experiences they had earlier in their life being formative for many aspects of their working life.

Have you any early-life experiences that have contributed to your views or experience of resilience? Another way of thinking about resilience is to identify a time in your life when you have experienced a setback or some misfortune. Give some thought to what the setback was, what happened and how you dealt with it. Make some notes as we will revisit this in the next section.

Having good-quality, supportive relationships with people who can support and help you, a positive mental attitude overall, good levels of self-belief and self-confidence all contribute to your ability to be resilient and influence how you deal with life's challenges and misfortunes. In addition to this, it is important to work for an organisation that takes employees' well-being seriously and offers support and initiatives to help their employees to thrive. Having good resilience is important for both individuals and organisations because:

- it contributes to your overall well-being
- it will help you to deal with and recover from the setbacks that life presents
- it helps you to grow and develop
- it improves your feelings of self-worth and belief
- it contributes towards your general levels of optimism and positivity
- it helps you to deal with pressure and stress in an effective way
- it contributes to an individual's enjoyment of their work and their performance in their job
- it tends to lead to lower levels of sickness, time off work and staff turnover.

Key capabilities of relational resilience

In our view there are certain key capabilities or features that contribute to a person's overall resilience. These are illustrated in the chart below.

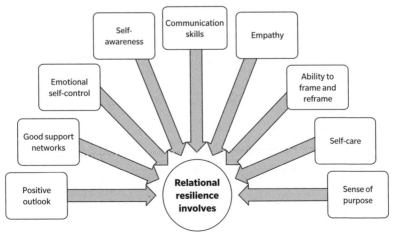

Before we start exploring what each of these features means you might like to assess your view of your own resilience. Look at the statements below and assess yourself on a scale of 1 – not at all like me to 5 – very like me.

	Score
1 I tend to have a positive outlook on life.	1 2 3 4 5
2 I tend to cope well when times are tough.	1 2 3 4 5
3 I have a range of people that I feel able to talk to about life's setbacks.	1 2 3 4 5
4 I believe I have a good level of emotional control in challenging times.	1 2 3 4 5
5 I learn from challenging situations and apply the learning in future circumstances.	1 2 3 4 5
6 I like change and deal well with new ways of working.	1 2 3 4 5
7 I am aware of what makes me feel pressured and stressed.	1 2 3 4 5
8 I can talk about my feelings when I am feeling stressed.	1 2 3 4 5
9 I take account of others feelings when in a stressful situation.	1 2 3 4 5
10 I am perceptive about other people's feelings.	1 2 3 4 5
11 I can adapt my approach to a challenging situation by reframing to be able to learn from it.	1 2 3 4 5
12 I have a good level of well-being in terms of sleep, exercise and a healthy diet.	1 2 3 4 5
13 I have a real sense of meaning in my life and feel what I do adds value.	1 2 3 4 5
Total score	

If your score is mainly 4s and 5s then you are already quite resilient; however, that does not mean you cannot continue to develop your resilience. If your scores are at the lower end then you will find it useful to develop your skills and abilities to be able to be more resilient in the future. If you have a mixed range of scores, you might find it helpful to focus on developing in the items where you scored low.

Now that you have a general feeling for your current level of resilience you can begin to further develop your approach. The following are what we believe to be some of the key capabilities that can contribute to improving how resilient you are.

- Having a generally optimistic and **positive outlook** is probably one of the most cited features of resilient people. Often people who have experienced an extreme setback talk about how their overall attitude of positivity has helped them to deal with the setback and come through it stronger. People like this tend to be described as those who have a 'glass half full' attitude to life. They will see the opportunities in a situation and will learn from any challenge or setback. Positive people tend to take responsibility for their actions and behaviour and recognise that they largely hold their destiny in their own hands.

- The value of good-quality, trusted relationships to provide a **support network** in times of adversity is another frequently mentioned feature of resilient people: having a range of strategic relationships as your 'go to' people when in times of pressure and stress – a trusted colleague, friend or family member with whom you know you can honestly discuss your feelings and thoughts about any setback you are facing. The intention is not for this person to give you answers, but to be someone you can share with and who will be there to help you through the situation and move forward stronger. The old saying 'a problem shared is a problem halved' is perhaps appropriate here. Who is in your support network? Who can you turn to for support when things get tough?

- The increased awareness of the importance of emotional intelligence in the workplace has contributed to the issue of personal resilience, especially in relation to **emotional self-control**.

Emotional self-control is largely about recognising, naming and regulating your emotions. Taking control of your emotional responses and reactions when handling problems, challenges and failures can contribute towards your overall well-being, your performance on your job, your handling of relationships and your levels of resilience.

- **Self-awareness** in general will play a major role in resilience. Being aware of how others perceive you by getting feedback from a variety of sources about certain topics will give you a better understanding of how you might react in various challenging and problematic situations and environments regarding things like:
  - what you do well and not so well
  - what your strengths and weaknesses are
  - how others perceive you
  - what causes you to feel under pressure and stressed.

- Focussing on, developing and deploying effective **communication skills** including active listening, questioning, summarising, testing understanding and non-verbal behaviour all contribute to your overall effectiveness and to how you deal with the sort of situation/s that cause a person to call upon their reservoir of resilience. If you can use these skills to fully understand a situation, you are far more likely to be able to work your way through it and move forward in a positive manner.

- Having the ability to feel **empathy** towards others where you can 'stand in their shoes' will help you to manage relationships in a positive way where you do not rush to judge. Rather, you can explore and reflect about the behaviour you are experiencing and then flex and adapt your responses accordingly.

- Having the **ability to frame and reframe** situations and behaviour will help you to change the way you think about a situation. For instance, when dealing with a stressful situation you might think 'I am never going to be able to deal with this'. But, by reframing your self-talk and thus the situation to something more positive like 'I've dealt with situations like this previously so really this shouldn't be so difficult' you then draw upon previous experience and use different, more resilient behaviour and processes.

- **Taking care of yourself** is probably one the most important contributors to your ability to be resilient. Developing tactics and practices of self-care such as good-quality and regular sleep, exercise, eating well and practising relaxation techniques such as mindfulness and meditation will help you build your resilience so that you can deal effectively with adversity, challenges, trauma and stress. What do you do to take care of yourself?

- Having a **sense of purpose** where you know what you are striving for and what gives your life meaning will help you stay strong and enable you to deal effectively with tough situations. What is your purpose? Consider what's important in your life, what your values are, what makes you happy and what you are good at.

Building and developing your resilience

The theory of positive psychology has contributed much to the development of an individual's level of resilience. Positive psychology examines how people thrive and grow and how they can lead a contented and satisfying life. In essence it is about what makes people happy. In the context of resilience, we know that happy and positive people are far more likely to have good reserves of resilience and consequently a good ability to bounce back in times of adversity and challenge.

One of the contributing factors to both positive psychology and to happy people is the level of appreciation they have received throughout their lives. People who have had experience of receiving positive affirmations from others on a regular basis are far more likely to have reserves of resilience that will help them to cope in times of challenge and adversity. Not only that, but the people who have the skill and inclination to take the time to show appreciation to others will contribute to an environment and culture of positivity. This of course does not mean that negative feedback should be avoided, but you have to think about how and when you deliver it to others. In positive psychology circles the rule of thumb is to make sure you deliver appreciation five times more frequently than you deliver negative feedback: the five to one rule.

Showing appreciation does not have to mean big gestures; it is the everyday things that you notice about people and want to compliment them on. For instance, when someone makes a good contribution at a meeting, tell them as soon after the event as possible, but not only by saying 'well done' – actually tell them what you appreciated about their contribution: 'Jenny, I'd like to thank you for your contribution yesterday at our team meeting. Your presentation was spot on, I was also particularly impressed with the way that you dealt with all the questions and didn't shy away from the more challenging ones. Admitting when you don't have the answer but saying you'll find out and get back to them is very skilful'. Giving feedback in this way demonstrates that you really do care. Many people would simply say thank you or worse still, not even mention it at all. By developing the skill of showing appreciation to others on a regular basis you will model behaviour for others and contribute towards a more positive environment and culture.

You could now look back at the resilience exercise you did earlier and identify a couple of areas where you feel you are vulnerable to stress and pressure (those things where you scored 3 or less) and focus on developing in these areas. In addition, think about what helps you to relax and turn off. By understanding what works for you, especially those things that are totally absorbing and help you to block work out, you can then begin to build these and other strategies into your life so that you have effective ways of coping when things get tough. We all have different ways of doing this; for example going for a walk or run, practising meditation, doing yoga, going to the gym, going on a cycle ride, reading, listening to music or watching a good movie, to mention but few.

The role the organisation plays

Your workplace will play an important role in helping you to build and develop your levels of resilience. A transparent and supportive organisational culture that has clearly defined, shared values and beliefs where you feel the managers and leaders are there for you will contribute to how you deal with challenges, pressure and stress and will ultimately contribute to your level of resilience. In addition, an organisation that provides you with regular performance review discussions, appropriate training for your job and has clearly defined employee well-being policies will be more supportive.

The benefits to the organisation for their investment in you are a resilient and productive workforce; engaged, satisfied and motivated people; and staff who have good-quality relationships with their colleagues.

Finally

You are not alone with the need to develop your level of resilience; it has also been the key to success for many well-known people:

'Rock bottom became the solid foundation in which I rebuilt my life.'

J.K. Rowling

'It's fine to celebrate success but it is more important to heed the lessons of failure.'

Bill Gates

'Turn your wounds into wisdom.'

Oprah Winfrey

'Our greatest glory is not in never falling, but in rising every time we fall.'

Confucius

chapter 6

Why trust is a powerful driver in every good relationship

'The foundation stone for creating a positive and flexible culture is trust . . .'

John Williams, CEO of Agile Business Consortium; author of 'Trust is the Foundation of Business', *HR Magazine*, April 2019

Some of us are fortunate enough to work in a great environment where high levels of trust exist with our colleagues, our boss and more widely with people we interact with on a regular basis. Most of us, however, live in a more nuanced world of work. Certainly, some relationships are excellent but elsewhere this may be far less true. This, in turn, means that we feel wary about these people; uncertain about how much, if at all, we should trust them.

We will explore in this chapter how you can develop and maintain trust with others, as well as helping you to recognise two very different workplaces: one in which there are low levels of trust and one in which high levels of trust exist – the place where everyone can thrive.

Trust is often overlooked in work relationships, though in reality it is crucial. Lack of trust is often at the heart of a dysfunctional team – creating too much ego, competition and jostling for power and prestige (combined with low commitment to the team). One of the most important qualities for any new colleague, and in particular for a new boss, is to establish that they are trustworthy: that those around them can rely upon what is said. It is after all the basis for any good marriage and the workplace is no different. Without trust everything is likely to be more difficult.

The Edelman Trust Barometer has been tracking levels of trust (in the broadest sense) for many years. However, the 2021 survey data are startling as they reveal that for the first time, we (the public) trust business more than we trust our government. One obvious reason why trust in government has declined is down to the Covid-19 pandemic and the impact of those early, dark times with varying moments of chaos and crisis among political leaders. There also is everywhere the undermining effect of 'fake news' on social media amplified by a flood of conspiracy theories and demonstrations by antivax protestors (as in Greece, Los Angeles, France and in London). Few of us can remember such dramatic events happening before in society. In fact, we probably have to go back to the Cold War (in the 1950s) and the Second World War (in the 1940s) to find such a bleak time for the nation and worldwide.

When people talk about psychological safety and how important this is at work, this largely describes the level of trust we have with one another. When it's low then this creates an uncomfortable place to work, people often will describe feeling vulnerable or insecure. When trust is high, this creates a workspace where people feel valued and secure: it is the glue that holds us together and makes work go well. When absent, invariably it creates more stress in those involved. Too much time playing office politics and double-dealing will create a toxic profession or workplace which can occur in any sector. It is often easiest to spot when you join a new company or team. There are various classic situations, listed below, about when trust is absent at work.

- 'My boss micromanages all of us in the team, he certainly never trusts me to do my job and is constantly checking up on me.'

- 'My colleague and I used to get on really well until I let her down one time. It certainly wasn't deliberate, and I've tried lots of times to explain this, but she simply won't give me another chance. If this was a marriage we'd be divorced by now!'

- 'It's hard to say that I don't trust my team leader – I simply don't know her and we hardly ever have any personal conversations. All she asks is about 'task, task, task', and a typical email arrives headed 'sort this quickly please'. I feel like a robot!'

- 'Our new boss doesn't get on with his boss, everyone can feel the tension in meetings – you can cut the atmosphere with a knife and this is affecting everyone in our team. We all feel on edge.'

Do any of these sound familiar? Most of us have experienced one or more of these situations (or have witnessed it happening to others). Perhaps the most upsetting is when trust is lost, as in the second example. Sometimes it comes as a total surprise. However, in coaching sessions we hear often that if a situation has been getting steadily worse over a number of weeks or months, there can eventually be that moment – the 'straw that broke the camel's back'. The colleague who won't 'forgive and forget' in that second example above had experienced a number of small incidents but decided not to speak out as individually they all seemed too petty. Only when this happened for the umpteenth time did she really lose her cool. The other person was completely unaware of earlier events until their boss decided to intervene and do some counselling with them both to restore trust. As key members of the team, such a falling out was gradually beginning to affect performance overall.

How does trust manifest itself? How can we develop and maintain it?

A variety of different trust dimensions exist across the workplace and it's worth considering the broader picture as shown in the diagram below. This outlines what we call **Connected Circles of Trust**: the first one at the top of the diagram is between the individual and the organisation, another equally crucial is that which exists between the individual and their boss. The one we have been talking about above is between the individual and their colleagues (or within their team). As you might expect, anything happening in one circle of trust is likely to have an impact elsewhere.

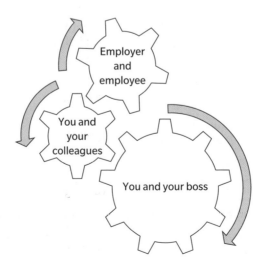

So let's take a look at each of these in turn.

The level of trust between employer and employee is important to both sides. The employer is only likely to maximise employee engagement with high levels of trust. One of the chapters in Richard Branson's book *Business Stripped Bare* is 'Find good people – set them free'. As he explains, 'If you are going to let people get on with and even develop their jobs, you need people you can trust'. He also has said that leaders need to be surrounded by people they trust. We wholeheartedly agree, but would turn this into a general rule: we all need to be surrounded by people we can trust.

As you might expect, trust is likely to be at its highest when someone joins a company and might thereafter drop lower. However, if the drop is too low then the relationship has become toxic. For example, someone may have a healthy cynicism about their employer: if this becomes too negative then it will break that bond of trust.

In the Edelman 2021 survey (mentioned earlier), the majority of people surveyed in the UK (almost 71 per cent) place trust in 'my employer'. Although it is positive, many large organisations these days regularly conduct polls of staff opinion to ascertain levels of motivation and engagement. They would expect to find higher levels of engagement. In fact, anything less than an endorsement of 90 per cent staff engagement is regarded as an early warning system likely to ring alarm bells at board level and ensure that an urgent review is made to address the problems and concerns.

The two other circles of trust are more personal, concerning your boss and then your colleagues.

The level of trust between you and your colleagues. When you join a new team, or new organisation, you will start off with just a few key relationships: possibly the people who interviewed you and a few of the closest colleagues you are working with. But then, you must know who to trust and this may not always be obvious. For this reason, it is important to take your time and build trust slowly. People have to earn your trust in the same way that you earn the trust of others around you.

The following six statements will help you establish whether trust exists with your boss, your closest colleagues or in your team. Answer first about your team:

Do you:

- Share information openly?
- Help each other?
- Have no hidden agendas (or power games)?
- Do not gossip about each other?
- Respect one another?
- Tell the truth and are honest with each other?
- Debate and disagree without resentment?

The more statements you can tick then the better the environment is in terms of trust. A team will not be effective if trust is absent, and often this is at the heart of every dysfunctional team you will encounter.

The level of trust between you and your boss. We tend to work hard at creating trust with our boss – for obvious reasons! If you are a boss, then you might like to consider the following description of Mike Henry, Chief Executive at the largest mining corporation BHP. His staff respect him, and he gets the ultimate compliment from a person who knows him well who says – 'Do people love to work for him? Absolutely.' (Hume, 2021). Consider, what would your staff say about you? Are you a great team leader full of energy and enthusiasm? Do people respect and trust you?

One key issue for any leader is to treat everyone fairly. If you have 'favourites' then don't be surprised if this plays havoc with the power dynamics around you. People will be quick to realise and resent these inequalities.

Another behaviour which makes a big difference with building trust in any of these three circles of trust concerns respect. It is one of the 13 behaviours noted by Covey and Merrill in *The Speed of Trust* and if you have ever had the misfortune to witness a culture where people are treated without respect then you will know just how uncomfortable and dehumanising this can be, especially if such bad behaviours are tolerated among those at more senior levels. The following examples highlight some examples of trust between the three different circles of trust.

Examples of what trust looks like

Relationship	+ Positive	- Negative
You and your Employer	Staff allowed freedom to set own holidays (as at Netflix: CEO Reed Hastings has said this is important in a creative industry where he knows 'some of the best ideas happen when you are on holiday').	A culture of presenteeism, in some cases from 8 a.m. to 8 p.m. or in the case of leaked comments made by one CEO in 2021 dealing with complaints from junior staff having to work 100 hour weeks.
You and your boss	Freedom to speak your mind and the autonomy to implement your own ideas, and to decide upon different ways to carry out tasks.	Micromanagement and in particular being closely 'watched' with a blame culture when things go wrong.
You and your co-workers, colleagues/ with your team	High levels of commitment and collaboration. The initial response is likely to be 'what can I do to help?'	When colleagues do not mean what they say, likely to over-promise and significantly under-deliver. The initial response is 'what can I do to help?' but limited follow-through. A key question to ask is: Does anyone care when you have to regularly work late or at weekends to meet deadlines?

The selfish gene

One of the most corrosive behaviours which undermines trust is double-dealing by those who, for whatever reason, are playing a power game. Always be on the watch for this as it often begins in a very subtle way at some distance from you: rarely is it played out in front of you. One classic example is someone who makes negative or disparaging comments about you to others (often those who are the policy makers or at a more senior level). These will question your commitment, your capability, your work or all three. By the way, this is far more than idle gossip; it's more likely to be a determined campaign against you with plenty of 'fake news'. By the time you get to hear about this it may be difficult to claim back your reputation. Published more than 40 years ago, *The Selfish Gene* by Richard Dawkins (1976), was a brilliant science book on evolution using the image that genes behave as if they were selfish. The same (unfortunately) is true in the workplace: the dark shadow side of some of the colleagues around you is that they may, for whatever reasons, be extremely and deliberately destructive.

It can also unfortunately be the case that such bad behaviour does not always come from a distant place but from someone close to you, who previously you thought was your friend and ally. Our advice about how to deal with this type of negative campaign is to tread warily with this person in the future. Make sure that you 'cover your back' by following due process: keep a paper trail of meetings, decisions and actions. You might also want to avoid one-on-one meetings with the person and ensure others are also present.

Some key characteristics of a high, and a low, level of trust in a workplace are outlined in the chart below. We'll begin on the left-hand column with a low level of trust. In this situation people are most likely to say 'I wish I didn't work here'. The opposite environment, one with a high level of trust, is set out in the right-hand column. In this situation people are most likely to say 'This is a brilliant place to work, I'm really proud of the work we do'.

Identifying high and low levels of trust in the workplace

Low levels of trust	High levels of trust
• Lack of respect for individuals	• Respect for others at all levels (not only for those in your own peer group)
• Limited or no sharing of information	• Sharing of information and ideas is the norm
• Ineffective teamwork and many examples of dysfunctional teams	• Effective teamwork based on collaboration and cooperation rather than on competitiveness
• There is a blame culture when things go wrong, pointing the finger at 'who is to blame'	• There is a learning culture when things go wrong with the emphasis on 'how can we ensure we learn from our mistake' rather than a blame game
• People have a poor attitude towards work, either being lazy or lacking in commitment. There is more interest in doing the minimum amount of work necessary	• High levels of commitment to work at a team level and in terms of winning at corporate levels
• Lack of fairness	• A strong ethos in both policy and practice of treating everyone fairly
• Evidence of avoidance behaviour, e.g. either not attending or turning up late for meetings	• Everyone is 'leaning in', keen to get involved in different work projects and there are rarely 'no shows' at any meeting
• People (at all levels) are reluctant to take responsibility for a decision; concerned that later they may be blamed for making the wrong decision	• People (at all levels) have the authority and autonomy to take responsibility for a decision. They are trusted to act in the best interests of the business
• A widespread culture of micromanagement	• Micromanagement is not tolerated and managers are encouraged always to allow staff to take responsibility
• You can perhaps add others to this list from your own experiences	

Does trust change in a virtual space?

The answer to this question is both 'no' and 'yes'. It is changed because in a virtual online environment trust can be harder to establish, especially if you have not had the opportunity to meet face to face with the people you are working with. There is also likely to be far less time (compared to office sharing) to establish personal connections and get to know each other well. Not least because your coffee chats and lunchtime meetings have disappeared.

One crucial aspect here is to be explicit about ways to create trust with one another. It is also true that developing trust across different cultures is likely to take more time, not least because it can be harder to establish our common ground and values. For instance, phrases, jokes or issues are 'lost in translation' between different languages. We will consider diversity issues in Chapter 8, but in the meantime think about the different groups below. How many apply to your virtual team or meeting?

Key characteristics of diversity

One of the key questions Konstantin Degner asks in his virtual teams' book is in the chapter 'Do you know your team?'. And in *Making Relationships Work at Work*, Richard Fox highlights the difficulties of working with different personalities. But it isn't all about differences; amazing change can be created by looking at processes and drilling down into how inclusive or exclusive they are. (This can be challenging if you are among the dominant culture or diversity so you may need to 'put yourself in their shoes'.)

In *Influencing Virtual Teams*, Osman Hassan draws on his experiences at Cisco with virtual teams and suggests you factor in different time zones when scheduling meetings, a simple change which frequently gets overlooked, not least because people may be unwilling to speak up. Or it is kept strongly anchored to the time zone of the person who is organising (and/or whoever is most important), neglecting those who are expected to take a call in the midnight hour or at the crack of dawn. (Another test of good processes is to question what you would do if this was for non-team colleagues as opposed to team colleagues.)

People in virtual teams (as well as those frequently using online meeting spaces) talk about feeling 'disconnected' and excluded in various ways from the rest of the group. One example is when the meeting is held in your second or third language. Try to make stronger connections – in every sense. In any online environment it is harder to read people's facial expressions and to pick up on those early signs when people are disengaged. For these reasons you often see more experienced team leaders who ask about such issues on a regular basis, making sure everyone is still involved and has clearly understood.

But regardless of what's different about trust in a virtual space, there are ways that it does not change. There are three key essentials that have already been mentioned earlier in this chapter which will help you establish trust online and to maintain it, as briefly outlined below.

- **Open and honest communication** – always seek ways to create a truthful dialogue with colleagues within your organisation and with those you deal with externally. In *The Speed of Trust*, Covey and Merrill describe this as 'talk straight'. It has a good deal to do with being collaborative and cooperating with others and establishing transparency, a process that invariably builds a great working environment. If you develop such a reputation for honesty, then this essentially is about integrity. Integrity is one of the key components highlighted in the article 'New to the team?' by Ruchi Sinha about building trust online.

- **Reliability** is also a great asset in building trust: by this we mean your own behaviour and reliability. In other words, be clear about what you are going to deliver and then deliver it. Reliability means everything in the business world. Again, if you practise this as part of your core values then people will know they can rely on you and this builds trust. No one finds it easy to work with those who over-promise and then consistently under-deliver or pass the buck. Similarly, if you are always the one with a personal agenda then invariably you will become the last person chosen for a team as you have a reputation for not being reliable. It doesn't matter how brilliant you might be in the meantime, reliability is often that essential, magic ingredient for good performance.

- **Relationships take more time** to develop in a virtual world (and require more effort) but are a crucial element of trust. One manager recently set up a 'Teams coffee meeting' to create a social space. But only one member of the virtual team turned up, and he only had five minutes before leaving for another meeting. Asking why people did not dial in, the response was predictable: 'we're under a lot of deadlines and work pressures and didn't have the time . . .'. Though one did confess she forgot! The next coffee session was scheduled in the middle of the regular team and client review meeting – everyone was already on the call and this has worked out to be much more effective.

Ways to make trust work for you

1 Consider one or two of your most important work relationships and consider the following questions on a scale of 1–10, 10 being the most positive.

- How much trust exists between us?
- Is there a shared level of commitment to making the relationship work?
- Can you discuss and identify higher standards of trust – and then, what would this look like on both sides?

2 Add 'trust' into work discussions at every level. Making this more explicit will help you build a coalition, and to identify different ways to build better relationships.

Tips on developing and maintaining trust

- Talk openly with colleagues about 'trust'. Make it part of work conversations and any review sessions; remember to regularly establish what a good level of trust looks like within your team. Consider ways to improve the level of trust between you.
- Consider the times when you just 'click' with other people around you and feel that they are trustworthy. Is it to do with shared values or perhaps shared experiences working on earlier projects? Try to identify the qualities and behaviours that are important to you in order to trust others.
- Imagine a 'trust map' and consider those workplace relationships which are low on trust – how could you improve the situation?
- Respect for others is a key component of trust.
- Behave with integrity; establish transparent communications, making sure you are being open and honest.
- Be reliable, remember to live up to what you say you will do. Over-promising invariably creates a bad image or being Machiavellian, playing politics at the expense of others or putting your own interests before those of your employer.

chapter 7

Secrets of social and emotional intelligence

'In this organisation there are too many people who lack social and emotional intelligence. This creates a good deal of selfish behaviour and generally a poor working environment. No wonder our turnover levels are so high!'

Director of a large tech organisation

Many of us will be familiar with the notion of 'emotional intelligence' which first became popularised by Daniel Goleman's classic book published in 1995 – *Emotional Intelligence: Why it can matter more than IQ*. However, it is still the case that too few organisations recognise how important EI actually is. In this chapter we will give a general overview of the different types of 'intelligence'. We will introduce and explain relational and emotional intelligence and how these can unlock the development and management of good-quality work relationships.

What is intelligence?

We're all familiar with the word 'intelligence', but not always clear about what we mean when we use it. Do we mean somebody is intelligent because they are a member of MENSA, or because they have a degree, or because they score highly on an intelligence test? We probably mean all those things, but we also mean somebody who understands subtlety, perhaps without having a higher education, or who can 'put two and two together to make four' with common sense and insight. It's a rather broad term and it's complicated by the fact that we're not all naturally 'intelligent' at the same things. Some people are more sporty, more competitive and excel at using physical skills to succeed. Others find written communication more comfortable than verbal, some people find maths and numbers come easily to them and others still incline towards pictures and images as sources of their information and inspiration.

So it's more helpful to think of intelligence as a process rather than a finite amount of something that either you have or you don't have, or you have more or less of than other people. Put simply, it's the ability to scan the environment, to take in relevant information and to transform that information into something useable. We can think about the process as looking something like this.

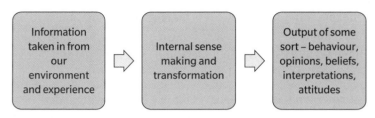

The process of intelligence

Types of intelligence

In 1983, Howard Gardner, a Harvard Professor and a psychologist, wrote his book *Frames of Mind* to try to unravel this complexity of intelligences. He proposed that there were in fact eight different types of human intelligences, and they were all based on how different people have different preferences for the type of information they first turn to make sense of their worlds. He identified the intelligences as

1 **Spatial intelligence** – The ability to think abstractly and in multiple dimensions. If you are strong on this intelligence, you are able to think conceptually, and in abstract terms.

2 **Bodily/kinaesthetic intelligence** – The ability to use your body, in sport or dance, to naturally use physical ability and skill to succeed.

3 **Musical intelligence** – A musically intelligent individual is sensitive to factors such as rhythm, harmony, pitch, meter, tone, melody and timbre. It may or may not include personal musical skill.

4 **Linguistic (language) intelligence** – Sometimes called 'language intelligence', this involves good literary skills of writing, reading, and using language to convey ideas, arguments and sentiment.

5 **Logical/mathematical intelligence** – This is the one that normally comes to mind when we think that someone is 'intelligent'. It's a rational, cognitive ability to analyse problems logically, and investigate issues objectively.

6 **Interpersonal intelligence** – This is to do with the ability to understand others effectively. It means that you are sensitive to other people's moods, can understand their feelings, and motivations, and see where their behaviour is coming from.

7 **Intrapersonal intelligence** – This one is to do with understanding yourself. If you have this intelligence, you are aware of and conscious of your own feelings, motives and concerns, and of the impact they have on your behaviour.

8 **Naturalistic intelligence** – The ability to understand the natural world in all its manifestations. Flora, fauna, the environment and our climate are the key sources of information for people with high levels of this intelligence.

So – where do you think your strengths naturally lie? Score yourself on the eight intelligences on the following table, where a score of 1 means that using that intelligence doesn't come naturally and a score of 5 means that it comes very naturally. Put a cross in each box to represent your self-score and then join the crosses vertically to complete your 'intelligence profile'.

Intelligences profile – self report

Intelligence	1	2	3	4	5
Spatial					
Bodily/kinaesthetic					
Musical					
Linguistic					
Logical/ mathematical					
Interpersonal					
Intrapersonal					
Naturalistic					

Although Gardner's work was criticised for a lack of empirical evidence, or proof, the fact that we are all able to score ourselves on a chart like the one above means that the idea does have some validity. It makes sense that intelligence is not a simple amount of something, like a kilo of flour, but a more complex mix like, perhaps, muesli. We all have a different blend of talents that make up our own 'intelligence'. Let's think about that in relation to how we can use our intelligences to ensure successful working relationships.

Emotional intelligence

Until about 1995, when we talked of 'intelligence', we often tended to be talking about the logical/mathematical type of intelligence. That is also called rational, or cognitive, intelligence, and is the capacity to acquire and use knowledge and skills, based on 'reason'.

That changed when Daniel Goleman's book *Emotional Intelligence* (EI), published in 1995, introduced a whole new perspective on understanding and predicting people's behaviour at work. Goleman had a similar idea to Gardner's 'interpersonal intelligence' but expanded the concept to include not only 'the ability to identify, assess one's own emotions and the emotions of others' but also to 'control those emotions'.

The Goleman model identifies four emotional intelligence competencies – see below. There are two inward-looking aspects or pillars of EI on the left-hand side and two outward-looking aspects or pillars on the right-hand side.

Goleman gave a descriptive name to each quadrant, so they pretty much do what it says on the tin.

- Self-awareness is knowing how we are feeling, understanding what triggers those feelings and using that awareness in our decision making. It means being realistic about our abilities and self-confident in a grounded way. Once we have acknowledged our feelings, and the reason for them, we can go on to control our feelings, which is the second competency.

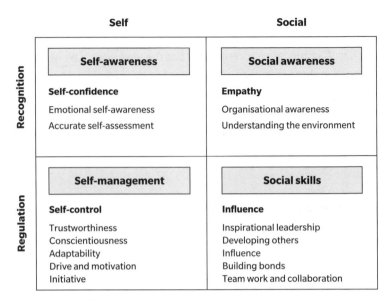

Emotional intelligence

Adapted from Goleman, D. (1995). *Emotional intelligence*. Bantam Books, Inc.

- Self-management means managing our emotions to help us get things done, recovering well from upsets and being prepared to wait for results – so we also need to understand here what results we want to achieve, our motivations, in our interactions with others.

- Social awareness, the third competence, is the ability to carefully consider and accurately assess other people's emotions and motivations, so that you can manage to meet both your own and their needs. This involves being empathic – sensing other people's feelings, needs, concerns and wants and understanding different perspectives.

- Social skills is the fourth competence and means using all that emotional understanding and awareness to manage situations, using interpersonal skills such as influencing, teamwork, collaboration and leadership, to achieve the outcomes that you need.

Let's have a look at an example of EI in action.

Terry was a busy single mum with two teenage children. When her eldest daughter (Sarah) was old enough to learn to drive, they agreed that Terry would teach her, in the interests of cost saving. On their first outing, Sarah said that she knew exactly what to do to start the car and move from the drive to the road and announced that she needed no advice at that point. Terry nervously acquiesced as she watched Sarah competently turn on the ignition, check her mirrors then quickly put the car into gear and hit the accelerator. Unfortunately, Sarah had put the car into forward instead of reverse gear and the car slammed into the side of the garage instead of going backwards down the drive to the road. The car was badly damaged, the garage wall was rubble, and they were both in shock.

Terry's first instinct was to yell something along the lines of 'silly child' 'wouldn't listen' and 'never take advice'. However, she quickly realised that to allow that instinctive response would further upset Sarah, would undermine her confidence, perhaps for a long time, and certainly put paid to the cost savings of Terry teaching her to drive.

So, what she actually said was 'Oh, Sarah, I'm so sorry. That's a horrible thing to happen the first time you get to drive a car'.

Terry's emotional intelligence on this occasion helped to comfort and reassure her daughter, prevented an escalation of the situation, and meant that they went on to successfully achieve the objective of Sarah passing her driving test with the least possible cost. They also had some fun along the way!

One of the reasons why Goleman's model is so powerful is that everyone will have their own set of skills and behaviours, which for them constitutes 'self-awareness' or 'social skills'. If the skill set or behaviours are appropriate, that's fine. It also means organisations can build their own specific skills and behaviours which they want to see as evidence of a particular EI competency.

Goleman evolved his model over the following years and, over time, he increasingly referred to 'social skills as relationship management'. However, this was always dealt with as the fourth component of the broader EI model. The emphasis of EI is on the ability to understand and control one's own emotions while understanding others' emotions and finding a way to manage both perspectives within the context of a specific situation.

We have argued in this book that relationships are the key to both organisational and personal success, and as such we are going to consider here that relationship management merits consideration as a form of intelligence in its own right. We're now going to think about relational intelligence as a separate, but related, skill set, with its own process of input, transformation and output, using relational information as the 'data' that we use for our sense making. Think of relational intelligence as a secret weapon in your armoury of inter-personal effectiveness.

The reason that this is important is evident in our working world today. We know that things have changed and are continuing to do so. Even before the Covid-19 pandemic we had realised that the world has become significantly more interdependent than ever. Many people have described recent socioeconomic developments as having moved us into the 'Information Age' where knowledge and technology are the keys to success. Now, where there is so much information and so much supporting technology, interconnectivity has become key. Like it or not we are now connected with other people in multiple ways – personally, socially, politically, economi-cally and environmentally. Global commerce, travel and the growth of global and multinational companies mean that these connections continue to increase, not only in quantity but also in importance.

Successful organisations, and individuals, must work within an ecosystem where their own technological platforms can speak to others, provide connected systems and meet customer needs in a way that has not been as necessary before.

At the same time as organisations are getting to grips with these macro relationship issues, the concept of relational leadership is beginning to hold sway. We've known for some time that the old 'command and control' style of leadership is rarely acceptable today. Senior leaders, who need to take tough decisions, are talking about the importance of leading in a relational way.

'You can only make quick, hard, serious decisions by putting in the hard relationship work ahead of the need. It takes time. Relationships are key. You have to make decisions with the best information you have, and that information won't always be "in" the leader.'

Senior NHS leader, November 2021

On a personal level, we know that, while we don't have to like everybody at work, we must have good working relationships with those we depend on to help us to do a good job.

Relational intelligence

The term 'relational intelligence' has been used by writers such as Esther Perel, in 2019, to refer to intimate, couples' relationships (see 'Esther Perel on Relationships & Workplace Dynamics at SXSW 2019'). However, the idea focusses on making connections and being able to develop and maintain them while working in a complex, ambiguous and shifting environment. We have all experienced how hard it has been to maintain high-quality, trusting relationships while working virtually, and many people have reported how the need for personal connectivity came into sharp focus during the pandemic.

So how can we understand, define and use relational intelligence? Before we consider a model for the concept, stop for a moment and think about two people you know, one a close family member and another a colleague, both of whom you think you have a 'good' relationship with. Think about what you talk about (when you're not focussed on a task together), what information you share, how you feel when you are with them and what value you get from (or give to) the relationship. Make some notes in the following table.

Good relationships descriptions

Family member	Colleague

Those issues you have been thinking about may align with our model of relational intelligence, which we have developed through research during our coaching and teaching practice. Like Daniel Goleman's EI model, there are four key factors. In this model, the information or data that we attend to are different aspects of our relationships, and we examine the four factors to see if we need to take action to make the relationship work better for the individuals within it.

Let's think about each of these factors in turn.

- **Purpose.** All relationships have purpose, but they can be complex and multifaceted. The primary purpose may appear relatively simple, such as to get a job done, or to develop the skill set of a colleague, or to work together to manage risk in the workplace. However, it may be much more complicated, such as to look after a child so that it can grow safely, feel loved and confident and

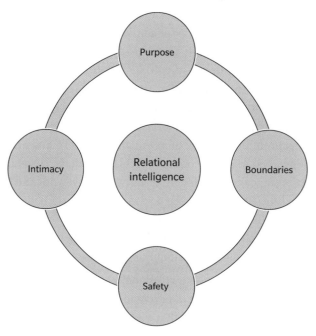

Relational intelligence model
Source: Author's own, 2023

then become independent. Friendship relationships may start with shared interests and learning, and then become important for emotional support. While relationships can serve multiple purposes, and can also be dynamic and develop over time, it's important to understand what the reasons for the connections are. It's only by understanding purpose that you can bring intelligence to bear on whether the relationship is functioning well or not, and whether you need to do something differently to make it successful.

- **Boundaries.** The boundaries of a relationship will depend to a large extent upon its purpose. We need to know those boundaries and what are the appropriate ways of connecting within them. There are several things we need to bear in mind when trying to be clear about boundaries. First, there are our social and cultural norms – or the 'way we do things around here'. These norms are often subtle and help us to decide what is expected of us within the boundaries of that relationship. If we don't give this any thought, we might 'overstep the mark' and risk damaging the relationship. Again though, these are dynamic and can change over time. A straightforward working relationship can develop into friendship and the boundaries will shift, allowing different behaviours and ways of communicating to become acceptable, and indeed expected. The other aspect of boundaries is of course personal preference. Some of us are great 'sharers' and are happy to be open and relatively boundaryless in many relationships. Others prefer clearer delineations between, say, work and home, and will be distrustful if those boundaries are breached. We need to use our relational intelligence to examine the boundaries of our relationships, check if we are working within them, if they can flex at all and if both parties are happy with where they are being set.

- **Safety.** When we talk about relational intelligence and safety, we're referring to the idea of psychological safety, which means whether an individual feels that they can take a risk within a relationship. In a psychologically safe relationship, it's OK to be honest about how you feel, to throw out a fresh idea, to challenge the status quo or to ask for help. To help you understand if a relationship is safe, think about whether there are any subjects you would be reluctant to discuss, any issues you would be fearful of exposing because of possible negative consequences or whether the other people in the relationship might have similar concerns. Unsafe relationships inevitably constrain positive development because they constrain and restrict communication. They create barriers to honesty and therefore it is difficult to have trust within them. If a relationship feels unsafe, it maybe because the purposes of the individuals involved are at odds or that the boundaries are unclear or have been broken or disrespected by people within the relationship. Whatever has happened, understanding again is the key to resolving the issues.

- **Intimacy.** The final element of our relational intelligence model is intimacy. This is the amount of confidence we can have that the relationship will contain positivity and understanding within the framework of purpose, boundaries and safety that we have established. While intimacy can involve affection and caring in a social or familial relationship, it translates into respect, recognition and regard in a more formal setting. This could also be thought of as another way to describe trust. Within a relationship that could be described as intimate, individuals will have a sense of security and confidence when dealing with others. They will feel able to depend on others within the relationship and will feel valued for their own contribution. Again, we need to use our relational intelligence to scrutinise this dimension to examine if we need to take action to develop it.

Now that we have considered the model, take a few moments to return to your 'good relationships descriptions' and think again about those two relationships. Try to revisit them in the light of the four dimensions of relational intelligence and make some notes in the chart below.

Then for each relationship, give each dimension a score out of 5 where 1 is 'could do quite a bit better on this' and 5 is 'really excellent'. This analysis should help you to understand where you could really improve the relationship and make it work better for you both. Make a note at the foot of the table of actions that you could take.

Relational intelligence dimension	Family member	Score	Work colleague	Score
Purpose				
Boundaries				
Safety				
Intimacy				
Total				
Possible actions				

In this chapter, we've thought about the challenges we all face in our connected and complicated world. We've thought about what we need to do to deal with those challenges – intellectually, emotionally and relationally. These challenges shape how we manage our roles and responsibilities, all of which have a relational dimension. The need to interact with many different people, from different backgrounds, with different expectations, abilities, interests and values, requires us all to connect and to act interpersonally intelligently. We've defined relational intelligence as a process that involves us using information about the purpose, boundaries, safety and intimacy of our relationships, with a view to understanding and managing them better.

We hope that you can use this model to guide your relationships with others, to build trustful and positive relationships in all aspects of your working life.

chapter 8

The overlooked aspects of diversity and inclusion

'Diversity and Inclusion needs to be something that every single employee at the company has a stake in.'

Bo Young Lee, Chief Diversity & Inclusion Officer, Uber

For many years we have realised that the world's increasing globalisation requires more interaction among people from diverse backgrounds. People no longer live and work in an insular environment; they are now part of a worldwide economy competing within a global framework. For this reason, profit and non-profit organisations have needed to become more diversified to remain competitive. Maximising and capitalising on workplace diversity is an important issue for today's leaders and managers and we have protected certain characteristics to ensure diversity in the workplace. These cover a wide range and are: age, disability, gender reassignment, marriage and civil partnership, pregnancy and maternity, race, religion or belief, sex and sexual orientation. We have legislative guidelines and safeguards to help us get it right in those areas and increasing awareness of newer, less visible differences such as personality differences and neuro-diversity.

This chapter is about the detail involved in creating an inclusive workplace where any and all types of diversity are welcomed and appreciated. It also considers the important question of how we can be sure we are leading in an inclusive way.

Inclusivity, diversity and hybrid working

The related concept of **inclusion** puts the concept and practice of **diversity** into action by creating an environment of involvement, respect and connection – where the richness of ideas, backgrounds and perspectives is harnessed to create business value.

The new ways of working that we are now familiar with, following technological advances in communication and the Covid-19 pandemic need us to reflect on how we currently manage diversity and inclusion in the workplace.

Many of us have been thrilled at the idea of 'hybrid working'. The idea of more flexible options for working, for balancing our personal and working priorities has gained traction since the Covid-19 pandemic and companies are adjusting to the notion that this idea is here to stay. There are clear advantages for many of us in being able to take advantage of the flexibility that hybrid working offers – we can tailor our working timetable, can choose to work where we feel most productive and, importantly, have control and autonomy over our working lives.

However, it's worth pausing to remember that there may be some hidden downsides to these changes, which may create new inequalities and emphasise those that already exist. Hybrid, or remote, working runs the risk of creating differences between those who are in the office and those who aren't, and these differences are not simply between those whose work allows them to make that choice, because of the nature of their work, and those who can't.

We know how important it is to ensure that the workplace is an inclusive one for all. To help people to deliver of their best at work, we must make sure that people are not only treated fairly, but that they feel safe and valued for the work they do.

However, the new world of work makes diversity and inclusion an even broader issue. It's about crafting a level playing field for engagement and reward regardless of all variables. Flexible working runs the risk of creating feelings of exclusion when employees are working from home, and of perceptions of in-groups and out-groups. The concept of 'proximity bias' is another cause for concern – this has been identified by psychologists as a bias on the part of some managers and colleagues that people are more productive when in the office, that they learn more from others and are potentially more ambitious. The counterpart assumption is even more dangerous – that those who prefer to spend more of their working time at home care less about their work, about being involved and have a lower need for 'belonging' and success. Whether in the office or on a virtual meeting call, individuals are keenly aware of how they are perceived and treated in relation to others. We know that perceptions of inequity can lead to divisiveness and feelings of frustration, isolation and perhaps even a destructive lack of psychological safety. These emotions have a well-documented and negative impact on both personal productivity and ultimately organisational success, while research also shows that teams that operate in an inclusive culture outperform their peers by an astonishing 8 per cent – so it's well worth working towards.

Creating an inclusive workplace

Let's start by thinking about what it takes to create an inclusive work-place. There are two key things that make us feel included at work:

- Fairness and respect – the foundational element. Underpinned by ideas about equality of treatment and opportunities.

- Value and belonging – individuals feeling that their uniqueness is known and appreciated while also feeling a sense of social connectedness and group membership.

Let's think briefly about each of those in turn.

The need for **fairness** is critical – it seems that people care as much about the fairness of the way an outcome is achieved as they do about the outcome itself. Remember that fairness is not the same as equality, so it's not about treating people identically – it's about ensuring that everybody can achieve the same outcome, by making sure that their individual needs to achieve that outcome are met. What's the process to achieving fairness? We can think about this in terms of three Es.

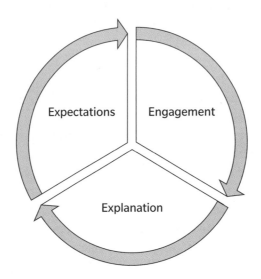

The three Es of fairness

Adapted from Kim, W. C. and Mauborgne, R. (2005)
'Value innovation: a leap into the blue ocean', Emerald
Group Publishing Limited/*Journal of Business Research*,
Volume 26, Issue 4.

- **Engagement:** Are people involved in decisions that affect them? Is their input sought? Can they challenge decisions made about them and their work?

- **Explanation:** Do people understand why decisions that affect them are made? Do they understand the process by which decisions are arrived at?

- **Expectations.** Once a decision has been made, is it clear what people are expected to do? What is different from before? What will success now look like?

Once we have fairness in place, we must continue to make sure people feel **included and valued**. For any business to be sustainably successful, it needs input and involvement from as many people as possible. Not only for the skills they bring, but for their diverse perspectives they bring. New hybrid working patterns can bring about specific challenges here. Changes to the way we work have changed our working identities and new relationship structures with subsequent changes in how we can bring our skills and contribution to the workplace and make sure these are recognised. These 'recalibrations' can create psychological pressures which are individual and need to be dealt with constructively. When many people are working from home, it becomes even more important to acknowledge the value that each team member contributes and that they 'belong'. Those who find relationships easy and comfortable will have little trouble working as effectively as before, taking advantage of virtual meeting places and social events to ensure their voice is heard and their views acknowledged – but for some others, remote working may emphasise feelings of isolation, vulnerability and difference. For these individuals, their lack of shared experiences and working directly with colleagues may make it difficult for them to feel valued, and this can have a profound impact on their sense of self-worth and their engagement with the organisation. As well as paying attention to diversity, it is more important than ever to ensure that the workplace is an inclusive one for everybody. When working together in an office, it's easy to notice if someone is having a bad day, struggling with a task or generally 'not themselves'.

Informal communications help us to remember that people have lives and relationships outside work that matter very much. When we don't have access to quick chats in the corridor or over a coffee we might miss symptoms of stress, anxiety or loneliness that might become serious if ignored.

To guard against this, and to keep relationships healthy, we must ask ourselves what we are doing to create an inclusive, safe and healthy workplace. In the office this obviously includes the quality and safety of the physical environment, as well as the psychological environment, but for remote working we must give additional emphasis to the latter.

Psychological safety

In 2012 a group of Google employees set out to investigate what makes some teams successful while others fail (the *New York Times*, 2016). They named their project after Aristotle because of his famous quotation 'the whole is greater than the sum of its parts'. They examined whether successful teams were made up of shy or outgoing individuals, those with similar interests or those who socialised together out of work. They looked at whether groups of 'clever' or 'average' intelligence worked best. However, despite the breadth of the research, none of the factors provided a clear indicator for team success.

What did the project conclude? The most important factor contributing to a team's effectiveness had nothing to do with the intelligence, experience or enthusiasm of its members. Instead, success lay in how co-workers related to each other. The key ingredient was something called 'psychological safety'.

The researchers concluded that 'Psychological safety refers to an individual's perception of taking a risk, and the response his or her teammates will have to taking that risk'. This means that in a psychologically safe team no one will find it difficult to offer a fresh idea, to ask for help or critically to challenge the status quo. After studying the group for a year, the researchers concluded that being able to have a voice and to influence the group was key. To keep working relationships healthy and to ensure inclusion, it's important to check the psychological safety of our working environment.

Google helpfully offered a checklist of questions to use to help managers to understand the psychological safety of their team. These questions can help leaders to judge whether their teams have strong psychological safety or whether there is developmental work yet to do. The following table uses the Google checklist, and incorporates the work of Abraham Maslow (1943) who first used the phrase 'Freedom from Threat' to represent our fundamental need for safety and security.

Each of the following statements represents a dimension of psychological safety.

Score each of them on a scale of 1–3 according to how strongly you agree with each statement. (1 is Usually agree, 2 is Occasionally agree and 3 is Never agree)

Then add the 3 sub totals for your total score.

Psychological Safety Statement	Usually agree 1	Sometimes agree 2	Never agree 3
If I get something wrong when working in my team, I worry about the consequences for me personally			
It is hard to have 'difficult' conversations in my team, or to bring up awkward issues			
There is a lot of gossip and rumour mongering in our team			
My manager does not prioritise protecting our team			
It's better to play safe and 'stick to the rules' when deciding what to do in my team.			

◀

It's difficult to predict what will happen in my team			
Asking for help is seen as a weakness in my team			
We are loyal to each other in my team			
My team members don't notice or value my contribution			
My team would really miss me personally, as well as professionally, if I left.			
Total score for each column			
Total score			

So, the higher the score (maximum 30) the more psychologically safe you feel in your team. The lower your score (minimum of 10) might mean that you may be experiencing levels of tension and 'unsafeness' in your team. A middle score of somewhere around 20 probably means your team has some psychological safety but could increase it.

Remember that self-assessments such as this are helping you to understand how **you** are experiencing your team. Other people may experience it differently, so as well as looking at the scores you have come up with, it is interesting to reflect on each dimension and think about what that means for you, and perhaps for the psychological safety of each team member.

Adapted from https://www.businessinsider.com/psychological-safety-assessment-no-hard-feelings-book?r=US&IR=T

To increase or develop and maintain the psychological safety of your team, and relationships at work in general, the other two E's we mentioned above now come into their own. Explanations and expectations both have communication at their core, and it is through them that we support psychological safety to buttress inclusion and value. It's important to remember that the responsibility for healthy working relationships lies with everybody, not just leaders and managers. Team members and colleagues all play their part and have personal responsibility for their own psychological safety and inclusion as well as for others they work with.

Let's think first of how individuals can use explanations and expectations to foster their own psychological safety. Two things are important to remember: (a) we must all take care of our mental well-being, by being relationally aware (using our relational intelligence) and (b) we must try to focus only on what we can control.

It may be difficult to jump into a virtual meeting conversation and have our voice heard. Here are some specific tips individuals can use.

1 **Encourage open discussion.** Stay actively curious about others and their different perspectives. Ask questions that invite opposing viewpoints. Listen respectfully to what others have to say. Ask people to explain why they think what they do.

2 **Suggest a bad ideas brainstorm.** This takes the pressure off trying to find a solution to a difficult problem; it allows everybody to be silly and adventurous.

3 **Ask clarifying questions (to make it okay for others to do the same).** When team members and colleagues (or bosses!) use acronyms or jargon, ask them to explain (and avoid using them yourself).

4 **Use generative language.** Respond to suggestions with 'Let's try it!' or 'Building on that idea . . . '.

Leading inclusively

As leaders and managers, how can we be sure we are leading inclusively and therefore getting the best from our teams, for our organisations and for the individuals? There has been a lot of recent research into what inclusive leadership looks like and there is agreement on six key qualities displayed by leaders who would describe themselves and be described by others as inclusive.

1 **Visible commitment:** They articulate authentic commitment to diversity, challenge the status quo, hold others accountable and make diversity and inclusion a personal priority.

2 **Courage and humility:** They are modest about capabilities, admit mistakes and create the space for others to contribute.

3 **Awareness of bias:** They show awareness of personal blind spots, as well as flaws in the system, and work hard to ensure a meritocracy.

4 **Curiosity about others:** They demonstrate an open mindset and deep curiosity about others, listen without judgment and seek with empathy to understand those around them.

5 **Cultural intelligence:** They are attentive to others' cultures and adapt as required.

6 **Effective collaboration:** They empower others, pay attention to diversity of thinking and psychological safety and focus on team cohesion.

These dimensions were published in the *Harvard Business Review* in 2020 (Bourke and Titus) and in the chart below there is a short self-assessment exercise, building on these dimensions and elaborating on them, for you to reflect on how inclusive your current leadership style is.

Inclusive leadership self-assessment – scoring instructions

Using the profile template in the box, put a cross on the line beneath each of the dimensions, corresponding to how you rate yourself on each dimension. The right-hand side represents 'Extremely good at this, other people see it, note it and value it'. The left-hand side is 'Definitely could do better at this'. To help you arrive at the rating, think of one, or preferably two, examples of the behaviour. If that's not too easy, or you need to 'massage' an example, then you'll probably be scoring on the left-hand side of the page.

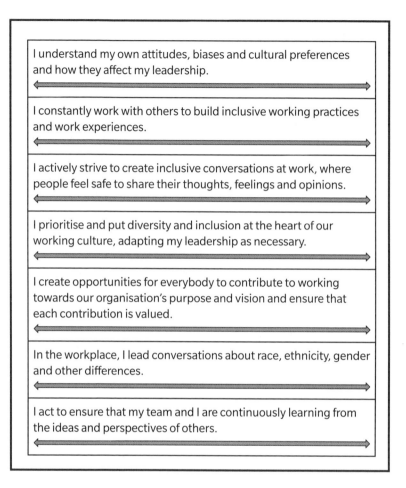

I understand my own attitudes, biases and cultural preferences and how they affect my leadership.

I constantly work with others to build inclusive working practices and work experiences.

I actively strive to create inclusive conversations at work, where people feel safe to share their thoughts, feelings and opinions.

I prioritise and put diversity and inclusion at the heart of our working culture, adapting my leadership as necessary.

I create opportunities for everybody to contribute to working towards our organisation's purpose and vision and ensure that each contribution is valued.

In the workplace, I lead conversations about race, ethnicity, gender and other differences.

I act to ensure that my team and I are continuously learning from the ideas and perspectives of others.

Here are some other tips to think about.

- **Create team agreements.** These are the expectations around ground rules for how you'll treat one another.

- **Ask your team how you can help.** If a member of your team needs help, it's your job to start the conversation. Ask them what they need and expect from you.

- **Balance activities with communication.** The work needs to get done, but teams also need to take the time to discuss feelings and needs.

- **Ask questions that get to a deeper level.** A question like 'When you think of your childhood, what meal comes to mind and why?' elicits a different response than 'What's your favourite food?'

Finally, what should we be encouraging our organisations to do? The switch to remote and hybrid working has brought about many changes to organisational structures and processes, some of which can be isolating and a barrier to inclusion. Yet, the hybrid model is probably a long-term solution for many organisations and so it's important that they find a way to design their workplaces, both physical and remote, in a way that has fairness and inclusivity at the core.

Let's think first about how people join organisations and are welcomed in as part of the team. Many individuals now have jobs and may not have met their colleagues face to face. They may not be based in an office and may have been recruited and inducted online. There are advantages to this – removing geographic barriers to where a job can be carried out allows access to a more diverse workforce. But newcomers won't have had access to colleagues who can informally 'show them the ropes' and it might be more difficult to fit in when everybody else seems to know each other. To overcome this, a buddy system as an integral part of the onboarding process can help, as can making sure that technical support is tailored to the individual and appropriate to what needs to be done. And just 'checking in' helps too!

To avoid feelings of 'us and them' if some people are in the office and some working remotely, organisations need to be explicit about providing forums where all can meet. A sense of community must be fostered actively with spaces for sharing experiences and interests that are not necessarily job related. Again, communication is key. Making sure that information is free flowing and transparent and that networks are strong and cohesive are both necessary parts of the new working world. The office party may have been much maligned in the past, and we're not suggesting a virtual replacement, but somehow the function of allowing people to connect and relate in a way that is not solely about work, needs to be served. Organisations must realise the importance of connections in making individuals feel valued, wanted and belonging in order to make the most of the new opportunities offered by hybrid working.

Lastly, organisations must revisit their recognition and rewards system. There has been, in the past, a perceived relationship between promotion and visibility. Often this is not a reality, but it is still believed to be a factor in many performance-related decisions. The issue of 'presence' is multi-faceted. We mentioned earlier that there may be a bias towards thinking those in the office will be more productive than those working from home. Yet often, home working improves productivity significantly by reducing commuting time and removing certain workplace distractions. However, the other side of that coin is that not all home workers are equally well provided for in terms of technology or working conditions. Another issue is proximity to managers – those that are seen are those that come first to mind when it comes to allocating projects and maybe even rewards. Organisations must be acutely aware of the inequalities that hybrid working can create and of the damage to working relationships that can be done if they are not addressed.

The rise of hybrid conditions in the wake of a mass switch to remote working has resulted in people spending more time at home, forcing a rebalancing of personal and professional priorities and changes in the way working relationships play out. We must all be aware of these changes and work together to ensure that our relationships stay sound, productive and positive.

chapter 9

Influencing is vital for credible and sustainable relationships

'Our minds influence the key activity of the brain, which then influences everything; perception, cognition, thoughts and feelings, personal relationships; they are all a projection of you.'

Deepak Chopra, author

Influencing and persuading those around you is one of the most important areas for success when working with others. Many people believe influencing involves presenting your ideas in an assertive, logical manner, with data and facts at the heart of success. What we have come to understand, based on research and many years of experience in working with people to help them to hone their abilities, is that it is a relationship skill involving both soft and hard capabilities as well as thinking about the best processes to use when influencing others.

In this chapter we will share our research findings about how people like to be influenced and what stops a person being influenced by another, introduce you to a process for effective influencing and help you to identify your preferred influencing style and how you can vary this style for greater effectiveness.

The crucial skill of influencing and persuading others contributes massively to our success when creating, developing and building effective working relationships. In addition, success as an influencer can contribute to your credibility and reputation at work. In this ever-changing world we have to be able to influence and persuade in such a way that we create collaboration, build cooperation as well as directing, leading and managing others in an effective way.

Take a moment now to rate your influencing skills.

The influencing process

Influencing is a process not an event. By this we mean that in most situations influencing is not a one-shot effort but rather a process which takes time and is affected by four key elements. The model below illustrates the process.

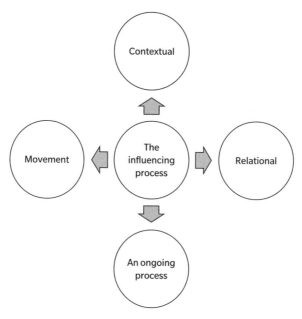

The influencing process model

Source: Brent, M. and Dent, F.E. (2014) *The Leader's Guide to Managing People: How to use soft skills to get hard results*. FT Publishing

The four areas you need to take account of are all inter-related and contribute to successful influencing.

- **Contextual** – every influencing situation you find yourself in is contextual or situational, which means you must take account of a range of issues before you begin any dialogue for influencing. For instance:
  - the people involved
  - the urgency of the influencing issue
  - the desired outcome
  - your role in relation to the issue – are you an expert, the boss or an interested party?

During this thinking or planning stage you can begin to give some thought to the skills and approaches you might use. This is often the area of most challenge. We tend to have preferences in terms of our influencing approach or style, usually one that is a tried and tested technique that you have found to work in the past and we rely on this approach. This is where many of us make our first mistake as, depending upon the context and people involved, you may have to adapt and flex your style in order to gain interest, commitment and ultimately to influence others.

- **Relational** – influencing is always about people, it's about convincing, persuading and gaining commitment from others for your ideas. Thinking through who you have to influence early on in the process will be hugely beneficial to your success in the long run. This will enable you to assess and plan the best approach and style to use overall and to identify when you might need to adapt or flex this to appeal to different people in order to gain their interest and to reach an effective outcome. It's also important to consider 'what's in it for them' (WIIFT) not what's in it for you. This is a mistake many influencers make. They get so caught up in their own enthusiasm for a topic that they forget that in order to be successful they must gain others' support and commitment. So always ask yourself prior to any influencing interaction 'what's in it for the others'. This also will help you to plan what you want to say and how you might go about it.

- **An ongoing process** – influencing is an ongoing process: rarely is it a one-off event. Many of the people you will have to influence day to day are the people in your relationship network and are often well known to you. Invest time to develop good-quality relationships and build your reputation and credibility with others so that they are willing to listen and enter into a dialogue with you. Patience is a real virtue here as many influencing situations require a staged process where you take your time to gather relevant information before setting the scene and beginning the more active influencing conversation. And even then, you may find that you have to adapt and adjust your approach along the way.

- **Movement** – influencing is often about getting small wins. It is rare that people buy into your ideas wholeheartedly at the first effort. What you hope for when you begin an influencing dialogue is to gain the interest of others, encourage them to ask questions, to offer their ideas about your influencing issue and to want to explore further with you. Sometimes these small wins will lead you to recalibrate your ideas in service of reaching an acceptable and workable outcome for all involved. Of course, this suggests that it is always worthwhile being open to others' ideas rather than being unbending in your thoughts. It is this adaptability and flexibility that gains commitment and support from others and ultimately leads to success.

Remember, influencing is not a one-off – it is a two- or multi-way process.

How do people like to be influenced?

We conducted research over many years to ask people from all walks of business life two questions.

- How do you like to be influenced?
- What stops you being influenced?

You might like to ask yourself these questions before reading any further. The answers can be quite enlightening. The best way of doing this is to think about a time when you have been excited by someone's ideas and have readily entered into discussions with them. What did they say and do that made you want to work with them? For the second question you should consider a time when you have been completely turned off listening to another's ideas. What did they say and do? What was wrong with their approach, style or argument?

From our surveys and research, we distilled seven key areas – these areas are as much about character and attitude as skill.

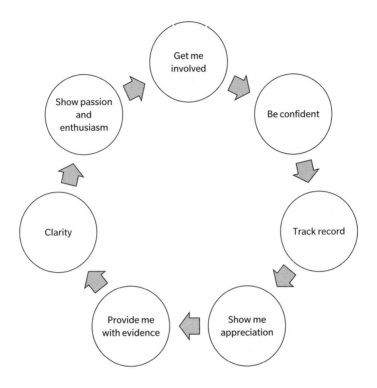

The most popular answer to our question was '**involve me**'. It appears that for most of us we want to feel that the influencer is actually interested in the thoughts and ideas of others and how they add to the influencing issue. This means that a truly effective influencer will be a skilful communicator using good listening, questioning, summarising and paraphrasing techniques as well as demonstrating a genuine interest in what others have to say and taking their ideas on board and incorporating them into the way ahead.

Showing **confidence** both in the topic area and the delivery demonstrates your commitment and conviction about the issue. This sort of confidence is more about energy, self-assurance and poise than about single-mindedly thinking that you have a good idea and others need to listen and take what you say onboard. It's about remaining open to others' ideas and contributions.

Having a **track record** where others regard you as credible and authentic with a reputation for being open and willing to work with others will always help to encourage others to work with you and give their support and commitment to your ideas.

Showing people that you **appreciate** them and their ideas will encourage others to enter into meaningful conversations and relationships with you so that you can work together effectively. It is also well researched that 'likeability' contributes to others being willing to give you a hearing even if the topic is a challenging one. A popular team colleague is far more likely to get a hearing for some unusual idea.

People also want to see and hear **evidence**; they want to understand the facts of the situation and the data that support these. Sharing your rationale with the people you are trying to influence will enable them to understand more about the issue and to ask appropriate questions and offer ideas from their perspective, which can add value to the end product.

Clarity in terms of stating your case and the goals you are seeking to achieve is vital. People dislike wafflers so, when influencing, take time to plan your thoughts and what you want your starting point to be and what you want to say – keep it concise and be articulate. Allowing others to ask questions will give them a chance to clarify and test their understanding with you.

When trying to influence others you must demonstrate **passion and enthusiasm**. If people do not feel that you are enthused about the topic, they are hardly likely to be willing to give you a hearing. Passion and enthusiasm do not have to be over the top. They can easily be demonstrated by energy in the way you present and excitement and knowledge about the topic and the goals you seek to achieve.

> *'Building connections to people is what matters when influencing.'*

> **And**

> *'To win me round an influencer has to find some common ground.'*

> **Survey respondents**

If these are the areas that encourage people to hear what you have to say and to enter into discussions with you, what are the areas that turn people off?

Turn offs or what to avoid when influencing

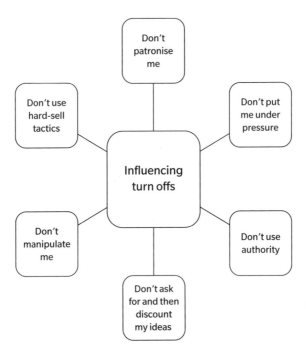

Again, our survey surfaced a clear pattern of the things that turned them off when being influenced.

- **Patronising** people by talking down to them and being condescending.
- Forcing people into something by putting them under **pressure**.
- Using **authority** by relying on position power.
- **Asking and then discounting others' ideas** in such a way that you appear to be wanting to involve them but then you completely disregard their ideas.

- **Manipulation** by misleading or deceiving your influencees.
- **Hard-sell tactics** do not tend to influence people no matter what the benefits. People like to be involved in order to buy in to your issue.

Based on all the data we collected and subsequent conversations with people from all levels of organisational life, it seems to us that there are three common themes emerging that contribute to influencing success both for individuals and teams:

- involvement
- clarity
- authenticity.

Influencing style and approach

Earlier in this chapter we talked about the contextual nature of influencing and how important this is for planning your approach and the behaviours you will use during the influencing process. One of the most important areas to be clear about is whether you require commitment or compliance. By commitment we mean engaging others to work with you willingly to develop loyalty to the issue and the influencer and to commit to the topic for the long term. Conversely, sometimes it is necessary to gain compliance; for instance, if there is a safety, security or possibly time-relevant issue. A recent example of the need to obtain compliance relates to the UK (and in many cases world) governments when they had to influence us to 'lock down' during the Covid-19 pandemic. Their approach worked for the majority of the population due to the life-threatening crisis we were living through. This, however, was a short-term solution to a much longer-term issue, and as time progressed the influencers had to deploy a greater variety of influencing approaches in order to gain people's longer-term commitment to social distancing, mask wearing and being inoculated. These approaches involved both data and appealing to our emotions in order to appeal to as many people as possible.

So let's look at one approach to influencing style developed at Ashridge Business School. Our model is illustrated below.

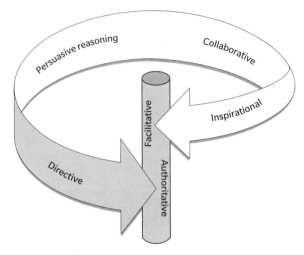

The influencing style model

This model identifies two predominant styles – facilitative and authoritative – both of which have two supplementary styles.

- An **authoritative style** is useful when:
  - you are an expert or are knowledgeable about the topic area
  - you have high levels of credibility with the people being influenced
  - you are dealing with a safety, security or time related issue
  - working with less knowledgeable people
  - you are well prepared
  - you feel strongly about a topic.

- A **facilitative style** is preferable when:
  - you need to gain others long-term buy-in
  - you are not the expert

- dealing with dilemmas and conundrums
- in times of uncertainty, you need to engage people's emotions and energy in order to stimulate their creative thinking.

Each of these main styles has two supplementary styles: **authoritative** – directive and persuasive reasoning: and **facilitative** – collaborative and inspirational. The important issue where style is concerned is to understand your own preference. Once you have identified this you can then learn about the other styles and how you can develop the skills to adapt your style to suit the situation, including the culture you are operating in. For many influencing discussions you will have to vary your approach to appeal to different people, contexts and stages in the process.

The chart below summarises the key characteristics and features of each approach:

Influencing style			
Authoritative		Facilitative	
Directive	Persuasive reasoning	Collaborative	Inspirational
<ul><li>Authoritative</li><li>Direct</li><li>Commanding</li><li>Dogmatic</li><li>Clear</li><li>Straight to the point</li><li>Confident</li><li>Expert</li><li>Prescriptive</li><li>Tell</li></ul>	<ul><li>Logical</li><li>Objective</li><li>Rational</li><li>Consistent</li><li>Methodical</li><li>Factual</li><li>Assertive</li><li>Focussed</li><li>Action oriented</li><li>Debating</li></ul>	<ul><li>Cooperative</li><li>Supportive</li><li>Common ground</li><li>Involving</li><li>Thoughtful</li><li>Empathetic</li><li>Relaxed</li><li>Curious</li><li>Consultative</li><li>Compromising</li></ul>	<ul><li>Passionate</li><li>Expressive</li><li>Articulate</li><li>Visionary</li><li>Innovative</li><li>Energetic</li><li>Eloquent</li><li>Animated</li><li>Feelings appeal</li><li>Creative</li></ul>

You might like to review the chart and mark up those features that you believe represent your approach to influencing. The column with the most marks probably indicates your influencing style preference. (If you would like a more accurate assessment, contact

Ashridge Executive Education Psychometric Services at Hult International Business School who can direct you to the Influencing Style Preference Inventory – ISPI.)

The following is a brief summary of the four styles.

- **Directive style** is an 'I' style where people assert their own views and perspectives on others who they then expect to follow them. They will clearly and specifically state their expectations often using prescriptive language. They will come across in a confident and controlled manner and will demonstrate knowledge and belief in their ideas. It is a straightforward approach where those involved know what's expected of them. This approach will tend to fail if used on knowledgeable people or if you have not established your own reputation and track record.

- **Persuasive reasoning style** is an issue-driven, action-oriented style where people use facts, logic and analysis. They tend to be well prepared and present well-thought-through ideas. They can be ruthless in debate and are happy to stick their neck out to defend their position. This approach works best with people of the same level, or knowledge or experience and people who will enjoy entering the debate. Failure with this style often relates to how you deliver the message and an inability to back up your arguments.

- **Collaborative style** is a team-oriented style where the main goal is to involve others through consultation and collaboration with others. In this style the influencer uses a range of skills including listening, questioning, testing understanding, showing appreciation, being patient and demonstrating empathy. This approach works best when buy-in is required for the long term, for instance during change, and when there is no clear path to take, meaning that the influencer requires thoughts and ideas from others. This style is the most popular style in today's business environment; however, over-reliance on this style or any of the others can lead to your failure to influence in the long term.

- **Inspirational style** is a people-oriented style where the main aim is to get people onboard by engaging with their emotions.

Inspirational influencers appeal to people's feelings by using appropriate language and body language. They tend to be highly articulate, confident speakers who are eloquent in their delivery, often using techniques such as metaphor, storytelling and imagery to get their message across to their audience. This style does not appeal to everyone as it tends to rely on big-picture thinking and can be light on data and facts. It can also be used by some for selfish ends and not for the common good.

In our opinion, no one style is better than another. The skill is in developing the ability to diagnose the most appropriate style to use at different stages in the influencing process. For instance, you might find that it is appropriate to start the process by inspiring others to whet their appetite to hear more. Follow this with persuasive reasoning to set out your view of the situation with pros and cons and then move on to the collaborative style to explore and work with others to gain commitment to action, possibly finishing with the directive style to summarise and agree actions.

Tips for influencing others successfully

- Be patient, remember influence is a process.
- Identify your preferred style.
- Be adaptable and willing to flex your style, opinions and ideas.
- Involve others by questioning and listening.
- Demonstrate understanding towards others.
- Be curious to explore with others.
- Show confidence and energy throughout the influencing process.

chapter 10

The power of healthy conflict

'Our director is a magician. She can gather any large group of people with widely differing and opposing views, let them have a freefall discussion but then knows the right time to intervene with a reality check. The review steers people towards realistic outcomes so the group can agree on a way forward, a consensus.'

Describing a Healthcare Director based in Europe

Challenging relationships and conflict are terms that, over the years, have acquired a bad reputation in the workplace. But if instead we call it 'diplomacy', 'relationship management' or 'good negotiating skills', then perhaps you can begin to appreciate how central this is to every work situation. We talk a lot these days about 'emotional intelligence' in the workplace but 'conflict intelligence' is equally important, describing those individuals who appreciate and value the power of healthy conflict as opposed to what often happens with negative, destructive conflict. These are two different worlds, as we will set out in this chapter.

Let's take the brighter, lighter world first of constructive, healthy conflict. This will add value to the business. Not only does it build better teams, it also impacts on personal effectiveness along with engagement levels for the company, as well as creativity. Instead of sitting on the side-lines being 'told' what to do, people are fully engaged with everything going on around them. In *The Right Fight*, Joni Saj-nicole and Damon Beyer describe healthy conflict as adding business value in terms of innovation and improved performance. We agree and our aim in this chapter is to outline the value of healthy conflict and help you develop such skills, including the introduction of a model for conflict resolution.

Negative conflict in action

When a negative environment prevails then the results often are toxic, as illustrated by the following examples. One person working in an intensely competitive organisation full to the brim with egotists talked about a situation where people not only stabbed you in the back but were quite happy to stab you in the front. He said that 'you simply got used to it'. A few years ago one senior manager explained there was no conflict in his company. However, before you think this might be paradise, the reason was because, 'none of our managers or team leaders like conflict and so we all avoid it, even at board level'. Unfortunately, this attitude is not unusual. As Patrick Lencioni highlights in his classic book on dysfunctional teams, fear of conflict is one of the five characteristics of such a team.

Elsewhere, people describe meetings where ideas are deliberately sabotaged simply because of the person who proposed it. There also are those 'fire starter' characters, people who enjoy lobbing in comments aimed at disrupting and derailing a project, often because they like to show off their superior intellect (and be destructive). Have you been guilty of either of these disruptive behaviours or do you work with someone who regularly enjoys doing such things?

Signs of a workplace with a culture of unhealthy conflict

- Competition and rivalry are the order of the day with feuds and personality clashes. Inter-departmental rivalry often happens.
- Bullying and macho-management are tolerated and rarely called to order.
- People are not encouraged to voice their opinions at meetings or on an individual level to their boss.
- There is little respect for co-workers and colleagues. There may also be a strict hierarchy.
- Constructive dialogue terms may be used such as 'we'd like to hear everybody's views', but this is rarely meant.
- Poor behaviour is not dealt with, often leading to a downward spiral of increasingly poor performance, lack of engagement and poor levels of motivation.

A world where healthy conflict exists is a very different place.

Healthy conflict

Challenge occurs but this is in a collegiate way without the loaded in-fighting and turf wars. Meetings are conducted in an open manner so that everyone present can contribute – teams enjoy the intellectual energy from a good debate, but it is all collaborative rather than competitive. What does such a workplace look like? We have set out below a few key characteristics. How do these compare to your workplace?

Key characteristics of a workplace with a culture of healthy conflict

- A willingness to create a culture of challenge and encourage people to voice different views and opinions. Seek to understand other people.
- Collaboration is the order of the day, not competition nor discussions conducted in confrontational ways.
- Constructive dialogue.
- Respectful disagreement and sufficient airtime allocated to such discussions. Less about 'tell' and more about 'let's share views' and then decide.
- A generally positive buzz where people are engaged and excited about their work.

This a good place to reflect upon your own conflict preference and think about the scenario more generally in your workplace. A few questions below will help you consider the key issues.

Conflict preferences: some key questions

In your workplace: Which description best describes your working environment? Is it a place of negative conflict or healthy conflict?

If you are uncertain of whether 'healthy conflict' describes your workplace then consider the 'elephant in the room' scenario. This means certain important topics are not discussed in meetings as this would not be acceptable to those in charge of the meeting.

Your approach: How good are you at taking the heat of a situation with a challenging colleague or in terms of dealing with conflict? Are you a cool thinker at such times or do you tend to lose your temper?

How would you describe your own approach to conflict at work? On balance are you:

- A conflict *'avoider'* or maybe an *'appeaser'*?
- A good mediator and master of diplomacy?
- Unstoppable in dealing with conflict and challenging relationships but prepared to be brutal? For example, do you prefer a win/lose scenario where you win at the expense of others?
- Unstoppable in dealing with conflict and challenging relationships but with a preference for a diplomatic approach? For example, do you prefer a win/win scenario for everyone involved?
- Some other description?
- Likely to use any of the above depending upon circumstances?

What does this mean for your own behaviours and attitudes towards healthy conflict?

In the rest of this chapter, we will look at a model for conflict resolution but let's first take a look at what type of conflict you may be dealing with.

How to respond to conflict

Different levels of conflict

The following figure shows three levels of conflict that you may find helpful to use. The first on the left-hand side is 'difference', then 'difficulty' and finally a disagreement which moves into open conflict and 'confrontation'.

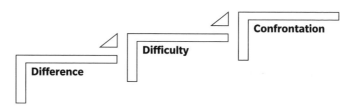

Three levels of conflict

People rarely spend sufficient time reflecting on what type of conflict level they are dealing with. It's hardly surprising really, as generally we are too action-orientated and impatient, yet with conflict it is very important to stop and reflect first before responding. You need to think about the model above – the three levels of conflict – whether it is about a simple difference, a more complicated difficulty or indeed if you are dealing with confrontation.

It's worth saying that all too often people talk about 'conflict' because it seems to be about competing views, attitudes or behaviours. We are complex human beings and often find it hard to work with those who have different values to ourselves, but if it's about such differences then we would describe this as the first stage of conflict.

First stage of conflict: if it's about difference

For example, if it is a difference of work approach, leadership style, values or personality then maybe you can begin to work out a better understanding or even see a straightforward solution. A few differences that you may encounter are shown below. This is not a comprehensive list, but simply highlights a few areas which often create tension. One obvious challenge is when an individual and their boss fail to understand and appreciate the other person's strengths. This tends to happen more often when a new boss arrives and 'inherits' a group of staff who they do not know very well.

Another dimension is between introverts and extraverts as well as, say, those who have a high tolerance for change (or for constant change) versus those who dislike too much (or constant) change. Others are:

- The focused planner who prefers to map everything out in great detail versus someone who takes a more relaxed approach, happier to go with the flow. If these are strong tendencies then both find it hard to work in their opposite style.

- The perfectionist takes great pride in their work and because of this may be uncomfortable to draw a line under a project or task even though the deadline is fast approaching. A perfectionist often finds it hard to let go and wants to keep on improving versus someone who prefers to keep to the strict timetable set out at the start (these people often make great project managers).

- Intergenerational differences are varied and fascinating: millennials versus older, more traditional workers, Gen Z versus Gen Y. And much more diversity exists and is relevant here such as age, culture, religious and gender differences. The key to this is whether both sides are willing to listen to each other: or, rather, are they willing to go further, to listen **and to understand**? The phrase often heard in such meetings is 'I hear what you say' but all too rarely this only means words rather than a proper appreciation of a different world view or experience. It's all about the willingness of making that connection authentic.

Sometimes these diversity differences are between employer and employees. One high-profile example in summer 2020 occurred when hundreds of Facebook staff in America staged a walkout (conducted virtually). These protests came after the death of George Floyd (the campaign hashtag #BlackLivesMatter) as a response to the tweets of President Donald Trump. Staff wanted a stronger response by Mark Zuckerburg and Facebook to stop the President's inflammatory posts and were prepared to take action to indicate how important this was to them.

Second stage of conflict: if it's about difficulty

Let's consider three departments with widely different views of how a project should be completed. In other words, each wants to be in charge. Clearly, this has now moved over from 'difference' towards 'difficulty' and challenge. The atmosphere is getting tense between them and there may seem to be little space for compromise. This is where it's helpful to have a third party who can mediate. If you don't have this support available then you must negotiate, having first considered the personalities involved and the power dynamics as this often predicts what the likely outcome will be.

The conflict resolution process outlined later in this chapter can help with this process.

Third stage of conflict: if it's about confrontation

In some companies there is a testosterone-fuelled atmosphere where bullying prevails together with 'personal turf wars and feuds some of which have continued for years'. Personality clashes become commonplace events and some staff acquire a scary reputation so that people avoid disagreeing with them.

One manager we know worked in their early career for a boss who was entirely confrontational; it was a place where personal insults and arguments happened most days. The boss was full of energy and drive, but also full of aggression. The younger manager had joined the company straight from school and so had no other leadership role model until a new boss arrived.

The new boss would only tolerate healthy conflict and set this out clearly to the team. 'No personal agendas or feuds will be tolerated; we collaborate and support each another. Debate is great but it must make a contribution to what we are trying to achieve.' He respected everyone's opinion and the younger manager described the impact, 'it was like a light bulb was turned on for me and I could appreciate how much more he achieved – with the same constraints, constant changes that always occurred at our site and often limited resources than my previous boss had done. I immediately wanted to learn this new approach. No aggression but instead a focus on getting the job done well'. The drive and determination were still there but now were centred upon how to engage everyone in getting the best job done.

When healthy conflict like this is encouraged then the workplace can be transformed into a very different place. Here the value of debate and discussion is recognised, though we should emphasise that we don't mean a fluffy world where there are endless conversations without decisions. The team, team leader or manager also understands when to make those key decisions and move everything forward.

Reflection/Review Thinking about the types of conflict you often experience at work, how well do you deal with these and are there ways you could improve upon your attitude or behaviours?

Are there certain colleagues around you who are good at diffusing confrontation and if so, what can you learn about their approach?

Smart ways to tackle conflict

In this final section we outline a conflict resolution model developed by one of the authors (Fiona). It is a practical tool which hopefully will help guide you through the process of conflict, whether it be about differences, disagreements or confrontation.

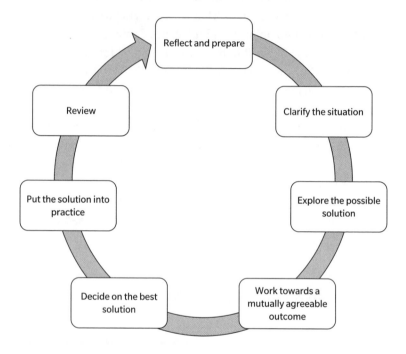

Seven-stage conflict resolution process

Brent, Mike, Dent, Fiona, *Leader's Guide to Managing People,* 1st edition, ©2014. Reprinted by permission of Pearson Education Limited.

The stages can be briefly summarised as follows: (For more details see Brent and Dent, 2014).

1 **Reflect and prepare.** Consider the differing views and the personalities involved as that will help you a good deal to antic-ipate what is likely to happen. We often find that people learn a good deal at this stage if they role play such a meeting in a

friendly way – find a trusted colleague, or your boss, who could help with this. If you have never encountered role play then this may sound like an unlikely way to help you. However, we have witnessed many powerful coaching moments when individuals use role play. We have, after all, too few chances to practise for such difficult conversations.

2 **Clarify the situation.** Is everyone on the same page or are there some assumptions involved? There often can be misunderstandings, especially if there has been a stand-off or temper tirade involved. Is there a back story going on underneath what people say is wrong? Summarise during these discussions and collect different views on ways to move ahead. It is important to have a clear, concise final summary that all parties agree with. What are the ground rules for the final decision?

3 **Explore the possible solution.** This should be a brainstorming session of possible solutions. The point at this stage is not to discuss the merits of each idea but simply to collect them all. In some cases, a more senior colleague will be involved – not just to help facilitate the conversation but to contribute from their own experiences. New ideas are often introduced that may help those involved to move towards agreement. What are people prepared to trade off or compromise in order to reach a solution?

4 **Work towards a mutually agreeable outcome.** The essential skills here are good listening skills and a willingness to hear other points of view. Working together in this way may be particularly challenging for those who previously have worked in an 'us versus them' environment. At this stage you may need to take turns, so everyone gets a fair share of the time available, but likewise all involved must be willing to make concessions. The key here is to create a two-way communication exchange, a dialogue. Try also to frame the conversation in positive ways rather than negatively rejecting ideas out of hand. No insults or trading off personal remarks.

5 **Decide on the best solution.** If you have shown empathy and respect earlier, then at this stage there is likely to be more synergy than confrontation in the room. Be careful not to reignite the

conflict by being either too assertive or overbearing – look for a solution that is acceptable to both sides.

6 **Putting the solution into practice.** The solution hopefully is now ready to implement with the blessing of everyone concerned. If you feel that you have 'lost' the argument then try to reframe your attitude and think about the value of finding an agreement and moving forward. There is too much emphasis in business about 'winning' at all costs, whereas healthy conflict reveals the power of negotiating to find a solution that everyone can buy into.

7 **Review.** Reflect on your learning from dealing with this conflict. If it's been easy, why do you think that has happened and if it's been hard then what could you do differently in future? There is always learning in such situations which if you take seriously the review and reflect stage, you can become more effective in dealing with such challenges.

Above all, you must be willing to change your views sufficiently to work towards a mutually agreeable outcome (in Stage 4). You need the right attitude to start the resolution process. If, for example, you go into conflict with a closed mindset then you are most unlikely to factor in the idea of creating a win/win solution. However, if you begin with an open mindset then you will be more than willing to put yourself in the other person's shoes.

Conclusion

Conflict is everywhere in business but it is never too late to change your approach towards making this a healthy rather than a destructive explosive event. Not only will this improve your communication skills and diplomacy, but there are other added benefits. Not least is that learning how to manage conflict and achieve a positive outcome creates a more effective working environment.

A toxic place full of negative conflict is rarely a great place to work. Humiliation and insults – everyday occurrences in a petty tyrannical world – are tolerated. A workplace where healthy conflict, also known as good conflict, is the order of the day is far more productive. The power of healthy conflict is that the focus is upon the work in hand rather than personal in-fighting, rivalry and bullying. Often the style which prevails is set at the top of the organisation; so if the senior team inwardly focus on competition at the expense of collaboration then this attitude will cascade down across the rest of the business. We invariably model the behaviours that we see, but do remember – it doesn't have to be like that. Individuals can decide to practise good, healthy conflict.

Dos and don'ts for challenging relationships

Try in any challenging or toxic relationship to remember the following points to help you refocus.

- Emotions (and temper outbursts) invariably make the situation worse and the same is true of personal insults. Keep calm and instead focus on positive behaviours that will improve matters. Often such events are unexpected: they may arrive at 100 miles an hour and so staying calm is essential. If necessary, take time out and meet again when people have calmed down.
- Be brave. If the situation makes you feel anxious or stressed then try to distance yourself from that intense level of personal involvement. Practise logical rather than emotional thinking and try to get the best from such a difficult situation.
- Clarify what the problem is and work hard to find solutions. One practical approach highlighted in Christina Osborne's *Dealing with Difficult People* is working through a 'problem table' by setting out the following:
  - current situation
  - ideal situation
  - action (and timeline).

►

- Language makes all the difference – one example is that instead of a 'problem table' mentioned above, the discussion is about an 'issue'. Similarly, rather than labelling something pejoratively as '**your** problem or issue' reframe the words as 'how can **we** resolve this situation?' Language can diffuse rather than ignite or inflame the problem.

chapter 11

—

Maximise your personal impact

'I've learned that people will forget what you said, people will forget what you did, but people will never forget how you made them feel.'

Maya Angelou, American poet, author and civil rights activist

In this chapter we will explore what contributes to the concept of personal impact and how image management influences the quality of the relationships you develop at work and in life in general. Personal impact contributes towards the impression a person makes when they meet you for the first time and how that initial impression contributes to the quality of any future relationship. It's about how people make you feel. Our behaviours and actions when we meet any person will contribute to how that person feels about and perceives you and then decides whether or not they **want** to work with you, trust you, respect you, value you and so on . . . .

What is personal impact?

Before we examine how impact and image management can help you build and develop high-quality work relationships you may like to think about someone you met recently and how they made you feel. Were you left with feelings of wanting to get to know that person more or did you have negative feelings leading to thinking 'I'm not sure I want to invest time and energy in this person'? Give some thought to what the person did, said or looked like that made you feel this way. Use the box below to make brief notes about this.

Typically, in the early stages of any relationship, we tend to subconsciously ask ourselves questions like:

- What do I think/feel about this person?
- Do I like this person?
- What's my first impression of them?
- Can I work with this person?
- Do I trust this person?
- Do I respect this person?
- Do I care what this person thinks about me?

Our answers to these and similar questions will contribute towards our early impressions of someone and our attitude towards that person going ahead. Personal impact is the behaviour and actions an individual displays and the lasting feelings these leave others with. It's all about how you present yourself to others and how they present themselves to you. Think about a time when you recently met someone for the first time.

- What did you say? What did they say?
- The language used – think about the actual words and phrases.
- How was it said – intonation, pace, etc.?
- How did you present yourself/they present themselves – body language and facial expression?

All of these ways of communicating are saying something about you. So are you displaying friendliness, confidence, wariness, hostility, distance, interest and so on. A person's first impression of you is very important and contributes to the other's initial thoughts about you. It's part of the decision-making process a person uses to determine their feelings about another person and whether or not they wish to get to know you further and broaden the relationship with you.

It is very easy to inadvertently give off the wrong impression by simply not thinking about what your behaviour – physical, vocal and visual – is suggesting about you. The following is an example of someone we used to work with and the impact of his behaviour on others.

This man was a senior member of staff, he was very tall and always very busy. When he moved about the building, he tended to walk very fast – causing people to move out of his way. He rarely acknowledged people even if they spoke to him. His facial expression was serious and he rarely made eye contact. How do you think people who didn't work closely with him regarded him? Well – they tended to be a bit scared of him, thinking him to be aloof, arrogant, unfriendly and generally someone to avoid. When he was given this feedback, he was horrified and simply hadn't realised the impact this behaviour was having on others. He made a few simple changes – smiling more, making eye contact with others and greeting people by their name when he passed them – slowly people changed their impression of him. He was not an arrogant man, simply tended towards introversion and being self-contained.

Early impressions of anyone are affected by your:

- visual impression – your attire, your stance, posture and how you present yourself in general
- facial expression – warm eyes, relaxed smile, frown, grimace, etc.
- body language – hand and arm gestures, physical tics
- vocal usage – tone, pace, volume
- language used when interacting – simple and clear, inviting, inquisitive.

These all play a role in how you feel about another person and how that person makes you feel – this then influences the sort of relationship you develop with a person. If a person presents you with a positive first impression, we are more likely to invest time and energy in that relationship, whereas a negative first impression may leave you less willing to develop the relationship and it may take longer or in fact never get further than pleasantries or what is necessary to get the job done.

The diagram below illustrates how this works.

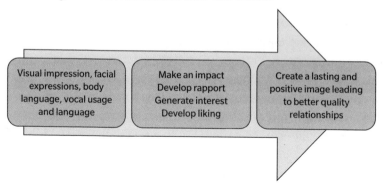

| Visual impression, facial expressions, body language, vocal usage and language | Make an impact Develop rapport Generate interest Develop liking | Create a lasting and positive image leading to better quality relationships |

Of course, there are no hard and fast rules in this area and what has a positive impact on one person may not on another. The important issue here concerns self-awareness and your own willingness to invest in using authentic and genuine behaviour that demonstrates appropriate impact and leaves people with a positive image of you, which will influence the reputation and credibility you develop with others. How others perceive you will affect most aspects of relationship management at work and in life in general. While we cannot expect to be liked by everyone, we can present ourselves in such a way as to be open, honest, trustworthy and respectful so that, whether a person likes us or not, they will recognise our credibility and value within the team, business or organisation.

Each one of us of course has to decide for ourselves about how we actually want to present ourselves and the image we want to perpetuate. This image will inform the behaviours we use when interacting with others.

Process for using impact and impression management to build relationships

Most relationships and indeed reputations develop in stages over a period of time. These stages are:

- instigation
- exploration

- developing depth
- integration.

At each of these stages we have the opportunity to demonstrate behaviour that makes others want to work with us to build quality relationships, which in turn affect our overall credibility and reputation at work. There is no time element to how long this takes: it can be speedy if you work with the other person on a day-to-day basis or it could take some time if your access to the person is less frequent.

Let's look at the key features of each stage.

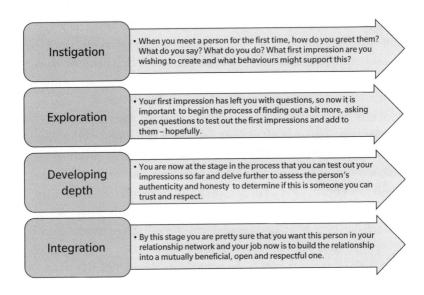

Think about a recent relationship you have developed and try to describe it by thinking about the process and the behaviours you used from instigation to integration.

Relationship being described – name the person and whether it was a negative or positive impression	
Instigation	
Exploration	
Developing depth	
Integration	
Make notes about any insights you have gained from this reflection. What can you take from this that you can incorporate into future relationship development?	

Until recent years most of us developed our relationships through face-to-face communication. Following the whole Covid-19 pandemic experience, many of us have had to get used to working online using video- and audio-conferencing applications and this has made relationship development and impact management more complex. Let's now examine how impact and image management can be built in the more virtual world we now all inhabit.

Personal impact and image management in the virtual world

During the Covid-19 pandemic, having no or little live face-to-face interaction was challenging for us all in many aspects of our relationship development and work with others. We have heard stories from many people about the frustrations of working online and the difficulties of establishing in-depth meaningful relationships especially with those people we have not yet met face to face. When working online we miss the usual cues and clues that we rely on to assess how a person makes us feel. It has been a steep learning curve to become comfortable in the use of video conferencing to best effect for managing our meetings at work. So we should attach some degree of importance to how we can adapt our behaviour to best create impact and manage our image for good effect.

It seems that virtual working is here to stay and will continue to feature in the business world and in our social lives going ahead. Indeed, many organisations are now looking towards enabling hybrid working – that is, splitting your time between home working and being in the office. What have we learned so far from working virtually and how can we build on this to ensure that impact and image management are as effective as possible when interacting virtually?

Here are some tips and ideas that you might find useful:

- Do some planning and be prepared. Preparation for any type of meeting is wise but more so if virtual. Think about the agenda and what you want to say – make notes. Think about who will be at the meeting, what you know about them and how you can best interact with them. Preparation will give you an edge and will enable you to focus during the meeting so that you can give of your best interactively.

- It is vitally important that you are well versed with the system you are using, how it works and what the features are in particular. For instance, how to mute the sound, video, how to use the chat feature and any other functions available – all very useful especially when in a group meeting. Lack of preparation about this can lead to failing at the first hurdle. This is especially true if you are the organiser of the meeting. If you are unfamiliar with the technology, it looks careless, thoughtless and disrespectful, leading to a less than positive impact with the others taking part.

- When you first sign in to the system, and best before you join the meeting – check how you are positioned on the screen – your head and shoulders should be clearly visible and you should be positioned front and centre on your screen – remember the others in the meeting only see a small image. Also be aware of the background – make sure there is nothing distracting or embarrassing – you can always switch on a virtual background if that is more appropriate.

- From a visual, body language and non-verbal communication perspective some things to be aware of are:

  - Your overall visual impression – what you are wearing and how you appear when on camera – hair tidy, etc. . . .

  - Eye contact – look into the camera not at the faces of the people on the screen. By looking at the camera on your device you are looking directly at the others.

  - Smile especially at the beginning of the meeting and always be aware of what your face is doing – you don't want to give the wrong impression by inadvertently using small facial gestures like winking, raised eyebrows, grimacing. Of course, these movements may be appropriate some of the time; just make sure you know the impact they might have on the others who are watching you.

  - Make sure your body language is synchronised with the message you are conveying, for instance if you are agreeing be careful your gestures and facial expressions are supporting this.

  - Vocal usage – don't hog airtime. Say what you want to say loud enough, using varied intonation, at a good pace and be clear and succinct.

- It's also worthwhile thinking about building in some social time rather than solely focussing on business. By allocating some time to 'catching up' you will be enabling a degree of informal relationship building into your meetings, which is especially important for any regular team meetings. This is important as many people tell us they miss the informal meeting opportunities that are a feature of office working – lunch in the canteen, meeting at the photocopier, water cooler, etc. Encourage people to share, for a few minutes, something interesting that they have done since you last talked. Be careful though that you do not overrun with this.

Be clear that you want to spend 10/15 minutes catching up then move on to the business agenda.

- Impactful interactive techniques to think about:

  - Use people's names – makes things more personal and enables people to know when you want to hear from them or are supporting their comment or asking them a direct question.

  - Ask questions; this encourages inclusion, shows that you are interested in the topic and helps keep things on track. Make sure that you are also demonstrating active listening by summarising, clarifying and testing understanding.

  - If you are the meeting organiser, make sure things are kept on track and to time – there is nothing worse than being in an online meeting and having people leaving because of overruns. This is frustrating for both you and the other participants.

  - Encourage use of the chat function (if available) for posting questions to be answered, support for people's comments and sharing any documents you refer to when engaged in the meeting.

- Encourage feedback at the end of the meeting so that you can actively learn about your virtual meeting process and especially what works, what doesn't and what might be worth trying next time. It is best to do this verbally by asking each person to share something that worked for them in terms of the meeting process and one idea they have for doing things better next time. In this way you will be involving everyone in developing how you and your colleagues get the best out of virtual working.

- One sure way of creating negative impact is to become distracted in some way. We have often experienced people checking emails, checking their phone or talking to others around them – all distractions from the meeting. You know what it sounds like and looks like – the quick look down at your keyboard and the clicking of the keys – both easily noticed on a video call. Some people think others don't notice the quick email check, but it's so obvious and quite off-putting and lacking in respect. If you do have to take time to check something, tell the others you are going to mute audio and video as you must take this important call, or whatever.

If work is going to be lived more virtually and you are keen to make sure your reputation and credibility are not tainted by lack of thought about your online impact and image, it is worth thinking about some of the above points and how you are coming across.

Use the box below to jot down what you think you are doing currently that has a positive impact and what you might think about to be even more impactful and inclusive. You might also find it helpful to think about how others behave in virtual meetings. What can you learn from those who do this well or how you think they might improve their impact? It can often be easier to watch others than to objectively critique ourselves.

MY impact in virtual meetings	
What I am currently doing well, e.g. bringing people in and making sure everyone has a hearing	**New ideas to try out,** e.g. build in more 'social time' in our regular team meetings.

When developing an impressive presence and maximising your impact with the people in your relationship networks, use the tips and approaches suggested in this chapter. These are all ideas we have either used ourselves or picked up from others when working online. It is, however, important to say that whatever you do in this area it is best to ensure that you are being true to yourself and reflecting your values and beliefs in your overall behaviour. Demonstrating a positive impact will also contribute to your overall levels of confidence and capability.

chapter 12

Consider what you say and improve what you hear: skilful dialogue

'A dialogue leads to connection, which leads to trust which leads to engagement.'

Seth Godin, author and former Dot.com business executive

We have talked a lot about 'communication' already in this book, particularly about the role good communication plays in developing and maintaining relationships. We know that communication is made up of many elements. Below is a comprehensive, but not exhaustive, list of some of the many things we mean when we say we are talking about 'communication'.

- What is said, what is meant, what it is the listener expects to hear.
- What is heard, what is missed, what is misunderstood.
- Non-verbal communications, body language, facial expressions.
- Art, writing, sculpture, painting, the performing arts.
- News bulletins, marketing messages, social media.

All these are representative of communication channels, or routes to communication, and we are sure you will be able to add others to this list, but we're not going to examine them all in this chapter. What we are going to explore is one of the most important of these elements: dialogue.

In particular, we are going to look at what we and others have called skilful dialogue – as we believe that this truly underpins the essence of relationships. Without dialogue of some form, some exchange of meaning which may or may not be verbal, no relationship between two people can exist.

What do we mean by dialogue?

It differs from simple conversation in that we use the term 'dialogue' to refer to a process of people talking through issues to build shared understanding and meaning. The key thing of course is the 'di' in 'dialogue'. David Bohm (2004) says that.

"'Dialogue" comes from the Greek word dialogos. Logos means "the word", or in our case we would think of "the**

meaning of the word". And dia means through—it doesn't mean "two".... The picture or image that this derivation suggests is of a stream of meaning flowing among and through and between us.'

We're assuming a couple of things. Firstly, that dialogue has a purpose other than being polite or passing the time – we're adding the idea of meaning or intent to a simple exchange of words. Secondly, we're including the notion of communication as a process – something ongoing that two or more people create together. To have a process that creates anything, including meaning or intent, we need to put some energy into the dynamic system that is involved, or nothing would change. Dialogue also needs an investment of energy on the part of the communicators. We could argue that the skills of dialogue are pretty much the skills of good relationship building – we need to involve other people and we need a relationship to be an exchange, not a one-way stream, and good relationships rarely happen without some effort.

We've already noted the converging skills we need to manage our relationships and interpersonal exchanges and it's pretty much the same with our verbal exchanges – they overlap. We all have many conversations going on at once. That doesn't mean we are physically talking to lots of people at once, but we have many unfinished and ongoing exchanges running in our interpersonal exchanges at any one time. For example:

- conversations that we haven't had time to finish
- conversations that need a little more information
- conversations that have piqued our interests.

They fulfil different purposes, and some are more satisfying and successful than others, but the more we can get them 'right' the more productive and fruitful they will be.

Let's see what other people have said about skilful dialogue.

The key elements of skilful dialogue

Two of the most important writers in this field are Lucinda Kramer and Isaura Barrera and in *Using Skilled Dialogue to Transform Challenging Interactions*, they have identified the three key elements of skilled dialogue as:

- respect
- reciprocity
- responsiveness.

Each of these elements are to do with how the people involved in an interaction experience it: how they experience being acknowledged, how they experience being valued in the conversation and how they experience being heard. Let's think about each of these in turn.

Respect

It's easy to talk about 'respecting' someone in a conversation, and we often believe that is what we are doing if we are polite and listen to what the other person has to say before voicing our own opinions. And, indeed, that often looks quite 'respectful'. But in terms of skilled dialogue, we are talking about something significantly, not just subtly, different. Respect in this sense means to explicitly and implicitly acknowledge the owned identity of the other person or people. What do we mean by this? Well, it's easy to come to a conversation with a preconceived idea of who the other person is. A troubled child, an overworked mum or a confident office colleague. This can happen almost at an unconscious level, so subtle that we are hardly aware of the labels we have applied to someone.

As we assign those labels to people, we are losing any focus on the relationship in the conversation, because we are, in fact, interacting with the label that we are bringing into the situation. We will then inevitably communicate with that label, not with the whole person in front of us. To truly bring respect into the interaction we need to interact with the actual person as they see themselves, not as we see them. That confident colleague may also be an overwhelmed mum, a guilty daughter, a jealous wife or a county tennis player. True respect means to honour the multidimensional nature of the identity of those we interact with – and that takes both energy and time.

Reciprocity

We generally agree that reciprocity is what we are practising when we exchange things with others and when both parties benefit from the exchange. This could be when 'you scratch my back and I'll scratch yours', or when favours are repaid between individuals. It's often on a one-by-one basis, although when someone says that the secret of a happy marriage is give and take, they are often talking of long-term reciprocity in the relationship.

When we talk of reciprocity in terms of skilful dialogue, we are meaning something quite specific. We are talking of ensuring that there is 'give and take' in the conversation or interaction, and that it is experienced fairly by the parties involved. For that to happen, each participant must feel equally recognised and valued for their contribution. There's something deep that must happen for this to be truly experienced as reciprocal. It's not simply to do with airtime or the number of times a voice is heard, but with how much value is acknowledged and attributed to the input of each of the parties. It's so easy to let the 'expert' voice dominate an interaction and for the 'non-experts' to assume their contribution is less important, but expertise is not the dimension that is important for reciprocity. To understand reciprocity here we need to acknowledge that while knowledge confers a specific perspective, everybody brings to the dialogue a perspective that is equally capable of contributing, shaping the conversation, learning from it and acting on it. Therefore, each person has something to offer that can create change, be of benefit to the 'system' and can therefore be reciprocal in terms of exchanging benefits – the benefits being those very diverse perspectives and conversational contributions.

Responsiveness

This third leg of the skilful dialogue triangle can only work if the first two, respect and reciprocity, are already present.

The easiest way to think of this dimension is to establish the difference between responding and responsiveness. We know how easy it is to 'respond' to another point of view by restating our own – perhaps more vehemently, or louder, or from a different angle. In essence, however, responding gives a response and acknowledges that someone else has contributed, but the response comes from 'my' position.

Responsiveness is achieved when my response comes from your or my position: when our responses both seek a connection with both mine and your positions but do not prioritise either. This aspect of skilful dialogue is all about connections. A good metaphor is a relay race, where each section of the race is its own contribution to the result but is entirely dependent on the others. In athletics, the diversity of fitness, skill and completeness will determine the result for all. In dialogue, the diversity of belief, opinion and expertise of the contributors will determine the result for all, but only if it is acknowledged that, although seemingly different, all the contributions are connected. This is quite a difficult thing to comprehend and it is about respecting all contributions and allowing reciprocity to be a dominant value; participants can then engage in responsive reactions to the people involved, not the issue on the table.

Let's think of another example: if you have a complaint or an issue with an organisation online – you are often offered a menu of 'FAQs' or frequently asked questions. You might find that none of the questions quite fits the bill for what you need to know, but number 14 is the closest, so you tick number 14 and get the standard answer to issue 14. Not surprisingly, it doesn't really meet your needs because an approximated issue is being responded to, not you, and you are frustrated and still have a problem. Real responsiveness hears what is being said, in a respectful and reciprocal context and is what moves the dialogue forward.

Here's a quote from Rachel Remen (1996) that really illustrates this well.

'So, I no longer have theories about people. I don't diagnose them or decide what their problem is. I simply meet with them and listen. As we sit together, I don't even have an agenda, but I know that something will emerge from our conversation over time that is part of a larger coherent pattern that neither of us can fully see at the moment.'

Now, this stuff is tricky, and we are not all instinctively good at it. How can we develop this and still get done what we need to do? Well, the answer really lies elsewhere in this book. The groundwork for skilful dialogue lies in the good relationship development that we have already talked so much about. Some of the skills we have discussed are what will move our dialogue forward.

One of the most important things we can do is to develop our **active listening** skills. These are often talked about as the one fundamental thing we must do to communicate effectively. It certainly is one of those things, but of course, if we don't ask questions, we have nothing to listen to, so active listening is the yin to the yang of **good questioning**, so let's think about good questioning first.

The essential value of curiosity

We all know the old wisdom of asking 'open' questions – and this is still absolutely appropriate. But for really skilful dialogue, our questions should not be driven by a formulaic reminder to ask 'Why' and 'How' and 'What' questions, but by a genuine interest in what the other person has to say. That interest is best referred to as **'curiosity'**. Remember what we are trying to do with skilful dialogue is to enact a dynamic process in a purposive way that will create meaning for all parties. To do that you need to be curious about what the other person needs from, wants and believes about the situation. Now, curiosity is certainly a skill that we can develop, but there is also an element of curiosity that is part of our personality, and that is quite difficult to change.

Impact of personality on skilful dialogue

The 'Big 5' theory of personality is the most widely accepted personality theory held by psychologists today and was validated by researchers Loehlin *et al.* in 1998. The theory holds that there are five fundamental personality traits that drive most human behaviour.

- Extraversion – describes a sense of exuberance and willingness to be involved and 'in touch' with the world around them.

- Agreeableness – people who score high on agreeableness are pleasant, cooperative and willing to compromise.

- Openness to experience determines an appreciation for newness, innovation and a variety of experience. It relates also to creativity, appreciation of art, imagination and new ways of thinking.

- Conscientiousness – describes how likely someone is to act with self-discipline, responsibility and an interest in achievement, to be self-controlled and reliable.

- Neuroticism – describes the overall emotional stability of an individual through how they perceive the world. It considers how likely a person is to interpret events as threatening or difficult. It has been described as 'the overall emotional stability of an individual'.

As these are personality traits, that is, they define a person's character and intuitively shape the way they are likely to behave, rather than being learned or habitual, they remain relatively stable throughout our lifetime. They are influenced up to about 50 per cent by our genetic make-up and to a certain extent by our environment. Importantly, research has suggested that they are known to predict certain important life outcomes such as education and health.

Nobody has an 'absolute' amount of each trait, but each trait represents a continuum so we can fall anywhere on the continuum for each trait. And it is possible to move our position on that continuum through consciously trying to be 'more' or 'less' of one or more of the traits. This is important if we want to develop ourselves in any way.

Exercise – Have a go at 'self-guessing' your 'Big 5 Profile'. Put a cross on each line, depending on where you think you sit on the continuum.

PERSONALITY TRAIT	Where I sit on the continuum
EXTRAVERSION	Low _____ High
AGREEABLENESS	Low _____ High
OPENNESS TO EXPERIENCE	Low _____ High
CONSCIENTIOUSNESS	Low _____ High
NEUROTICISM	Low _____ High

For skilful dialogue, and particularly for the curiosity we have been discussing, the most important trait is 'openness to experience', so let's think a bit more about it.

Openness to experience refers to one's willingness to try new things, to hear new ideas and to welcome imaginative and intellectual activities (Costa and McCrae, 1998). It is often described as being able to 'think outside of the box'.

People who score high on openness to experience are (according to John and Srivastava , 1999):

- curious
- imaginative
- creative
- open to trying new things
- unconventional and independent

whereas people who score low on this dimension are more:

- predictable
- less imaginative

- dislikes change
- prefer routine
- traditional.

Those who score high on openness to experience are perceived as creative and artistic. They prefer variety and value independence. They are curious about their surroundings and enjoy travelling and learning new things. We can see how being open to experience lends itself to that curiosity we need for skilful dialogue. How did you rate yourself on this dimension on the table above? Luckily, although our personality is pretty stable, there are ways we can mould and shape our instinctive characteristics to develop in ways we want to. Remember that environment and experience play a big part in our personality, and we can manage our environment in ways that allow us to mould the behaviours we want to exhibit. Here are some things to try to develop your openness.

- **Flex your imagination muscles.** This may not be something you do regularly so just try a couple of sessions of 'letting your imagination run wild'. Dream up a perfect pet, a perfect holiday, a perfect job. Or try playing a fantasy game or brainstorming with a friend an idea for a sci-fi novel. This might not come easily at first if your score was on the low side, but practice makes perfect and flexing that muscle once or twice a week will pay off.

- **Vary your routine.** If you scored below the mid-point on this, you may be one of those people who like predictability. For example, you might like a regular schedule and maybe always prefer to eat the same foods. This might be a comfort, but it can actually limit receptiveness to new experiences. Try actively to 'ring the changes' and vary your daily choices – making sure you look for any positive outcomes after you've tried it.

- **Keep learning.** An active interest in new information often comes more naturally to some than to others but this can really be developed. The idea of lifelong learning involves a continuous and conscious effort to notice new ideas, learn a new skill and meet new people. This can really drive the active process of openness to new experiences.

Let's go back to thinking about how to develop skilful dialogue – particularly in a post-Covid world when the contexts of our working relationships are more fluid than they used to be.

We have said that we need to keep curiosity and questioning at the front of our minds when managing our dialogue skilfully, but we also need to listen actively. What does that really mean?

Levels of listening

We know that active listening is more than simply responding to the words that are heard. It is a way of using our curiosity to delve deeper into what a speaker really means. It involves noticing what body language is communicating. It involves not interrupting and using silence effectively. It involves not judging or evaluating but encouraging and making sure that the conversation feels trusting and supporting. All of this sounds pretty complicated. A model that the authors have found useful during their work with clients has been labelled the **'three levels of listening'** and it provides a framework for us to practise active listening quite easily. The framework suggests that we should listen at a factual level, an emotional level and even more importantly at an intentional level.

- Facts/Thinking

  - What sort of words are chosen?

  - What data have been used?

  - What logic and analysis has been applied?

  - What judgements and opinions have been made?

- Feelings/Emotions

  - How are they feeling right now?

  - How did they feel at that time?

- Intentions

  - What do they intend to *do* about it?

  - What is their level of commitment to this action?

Try this exercise to help you think about your own active listening skills:

- Practise with a friend or colleague.
- One of you talks for five minutes on something important to you.
- The other listens for facts, feelings and emotions and reports back what has been heard.
- What levels do you find easiest to 'hear'?
- What levels prompt your curiosity?
- How did you get on with interpreting their intentions for their next steps? Don't forget to check this with them.

The key reason for developing skilful dialogue is that it really can be seen to improve the quality of our relationships with each other, subordinates, customers, suppliers and other key stakeholders, which is what we have spent so long thinking about in the rest of this book, and there are a few tips and techniques which we know are proven to help.

The first one is to make sure that we are surfacing and testing mental models – our own and others. There is much talk today of 'unconscious bias', and how we bring preconceptions to our dialogue that gets in the way of real understanding and collaborative conversations. The effect of these preconceptions or biases is to kick start an automatic process that occurs in our thoughts as we reach conclusions about what we are experiencing or hearing. We rapidly leap to knee-jerk conclusions with no intermediate thought process, as if rapidly climbing up a ladder in our minds. It can look like this:

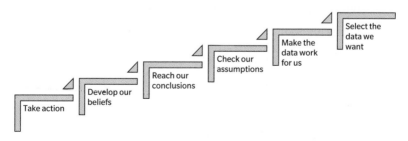

Based on Senge, P. M. (2014). *The fifth discipline fieldbook: Strategies and tools for building a learning organization.* Crown Business.

This is called the '**ladder of inference**' and is adapted from Chris Argyris' original work and shows how we can quickly confirm our biases, or hear only what we expect to hear, rather than engaging and skilful and productive dialogue. To avoid clambering up the ladder:

- Listen for conclusions or opinions – your own and others; check that they are not premature or self-confirming.

- Look for data. Ask what information they select. Give examples of the data you select to justify the point of view but avoid 'digging in' and simply justifying your position further. Stay open-minded.

- Make explicit the steps in your reasoning process and ask others to be explicit in theirs – acknowledge that it may be flawed.

- Look for the assumptions underlying conclusions.

Inquiry and advocacy

There are two key skills that help with this, and we can bring them to all conversations to avoid climbing up this deceptive and self-confirming ladder.

- **Advocacy** – involves clearly stating your opinion, idea or desire with a view to letting the other person understand your thinking. It shares the thinking and reasoning behind your point and engages rather than confronts others.

- **Inquiry** – needs you to genuinely inquire into the other person's views, at the same time as explaining why you are asking the question. It's a real seeking to understand, and of course to genuinely listen to the answers. For real inquiry it's important to be willing to experiment, and to hear something that you are not expecting.

Here are some ideas for questions that reflect good advocacy and inquiry in a skilful dialogue.

Advocacy	Inquiry
• Here's what I think, and here's how I got here. . . • I assumed that. . . • I came to this conclusion because. . . • To get a clearer picture. . . imagine. . . For example • What do you think about what I just said? Do you see it differently? • Do you see any flaws in my reasoning? • What can you add? • Here's one aspect which you might help me think through. . .	• What leads you to conclude that? • What data do you have for that? • What causes you to say that? • I am asking you about your assumptions because. . . • How would your proposal affect. . . ? • Is this similar to. . . ? • Can you describe an example? • Am I correct that you're saying. . . ?

It is sometimes useful in the beginning if you can bring in someone else to help you with this. We often see great results when there is a person to prompt, intervene and to remind everyone of these key questions, rather like a person off stage who prompts the actors when they lose their place in a script. Eventually it will become second nature to you.

Skilful dialogue is not magic, nor is it something only clever politicians or negotiators can do. We are talking of engaging in frank, open and authentic conversations that have a purpose and that help our working relationships to be productive and positive wherever possible. The starting point is to create an environment where information is fully shared, which helps the degree to which the intention to communicate is met. That needs to be where the openness starts, and from there we must move from 'proving a point' or 'prescribing a solution' to learning from the conversation. The **secret** here is to seek to understand and not debate or repudiate.

Let's summarise – to become a skilful dialogue practitioner requires a mind-set change from:

Non-skilful dialogue	Skilful dialogue
1 Assuming there is one best way to understand complex problems	1 Assuming there are different ways to understand complex problems
2 Assuming your point of view is complete and addresses the important aspects of the situation	2 Assuming your view is incomplete and misses some aspects of the situation
3 Regarding your point of view as a fact that should be obvious to others	3 Regarding your point of view as a hypothesis to be explored with others
4 Proposing options in either/or, win/lose terms	4 Searching for integrative possibilities that meet competing interests
5 Inventing ways to bypass others' options while getting them to buy yours	5 Inventing ways to test or explore options together
6 Minimising concerns and finding ways to bypass them	6 Actively seeking others' concerns and revising your plan in light of them
7 Discounting criticism as a threat	7 Using criticism to continually improve
8 Searching for data and views that only serve to confirm your opinion	8 Searching for data and views that might alter your opinion

There are few areas of relationship management that do not benefit from the application of skilful dialogue techniques. The idea of making communications intentional and working together to achieve a positive outcome for all parties is thrown into sharp focus when we think of virtual or hybrid working, when many of our non-verbal clues and cues in communication are missing. The good news is that practice makes perfect!

chapter 13

Authenticity, respect and empathy and success

'Authenticity is your greatest asset. Lose your authenticity and you've lost everything.'

Marcus Buckingham, author and business consultant

Being authentic and the idea of authentic leadership have become increasingly topical over the past few years. This is hardly surprising as not only is there more appreciation of the power of authentic leadership but we also now recognise the damage which can happen to people when they feel compelled to adopt a different persona or personality. In other words, being inauthentic.

The idea of authenticity at work is regularly referred to in many business contexts but what does it actually mean? In this chapter we will start by exploring some examples of both authentic and inauthentic behaviours. We will consider the role that values play as well as the power of empathy and respect in how we interact and behave with others at work.

Examples of authenticity and inauthenticity

Our first example is when a person joins a company (or call centre) where the emphasis is upon extracting extreme financial gain from customers with the least return. This highly transactional ethos, accompanied with a complaints system that is opaque or non-existent, can be challenging for those from a significantly different value system containing integrity, business ethics and honesty. Another example may be someone who deliberately steps into such a conflict of interests, such as the person who as well as being a member of CND (the Campaign for Nuclear Disarmament) worked for a military defence organisation!

Perhaps you have spent time working for a boss or a business where you do not 'fit in' or where you feel uncomfortable to speak your mind. This can happen when your views and opinions differ from those of the status quo or the majority and it can be both disempowering and stressful. Strangely enough, these difficult situations sometimes offer us the most valuable learning, such as the case of the marketing executive who told us he was suddenly confronted with a new boss who was promoted in above him. Quite apart from feelings of resentment, he was forced to be inauthentic as he disliked almost everything the new boss did as team leader. However, there was no way out apart from leaving and so he spent six months (until the boss moved on) watching closely and, as he later realised, learned how **not** to behave if he became a team leader. And in case you are wondering, lack of respect, limited communication, power games and autocratic leadership were a few of the issues he observed during those six months.

Similarly, working for a firm where there are few rules for how leaders behave can be a painful experience. Bullying and harassment are tolerated or despotic leaders are acceptable. Where complaints on such issues (even litigation) are side-lined or discounted even when a number of people report issues about a single individual or department. Unfortunately, some HR professionals may simply support the company rather than the right of individual workers to be respected and fairly treated. Instead, NDAs (non-disclosure agreements) are used to settle claims thereby keeping everything wrapped in secret layers. In such environments there may well be a public statement of company values, but we would describe this as 'fake authenticity' as it does not truly reflect the organisational culture or the beliefs held by those at board level. The reality may be a culture of fear, where employee engagement and motivation levels (whatever the company surveys gloss over and report officially) are poor. This often creates a high staff turnover. The tension of working in such a sterile world creates anxiety, intense stress, absenteeism and in some cases burnout.

The pressure to conform to what society (and organisations) expect is as relevant today as it was in earlier far more conservative times of, say, the 1940s and 1950s. In fact, one dramatic event more recently occurred in 2007 to the CEO of BP Oil when he was 'outed' as gay. John Browne had led the company for more than a decade and was one of the most respected business leaders. However, revelations about a gay lover and giving false evidence in court forced him to resign. None of his many achievements as an outstanding business leader could save him.

When, however, individual values are more closely aligned with the values of the business, we find genuine employee engagement and high motivation levels: a place where employer and employee, team leader and team members are in harmony with mutual respect for one another. It becomes a great place to work and to thrive.

Before we move on to consider 'what authenticity is' you might like to do your own self-assessment with the questions below. If you want a further challenge, then work with a colleague or friend, someone you trust, to discuss your answers and the differences between you. Fascinating insights often emerge from this.

Tell me, are you truly authentic?

Answer the following questions. Have you ever:

- Taken the credit for a good idea or the work of a colleague or your staff?
- Played one side off against another in order to get the best deal or simply win the competition?
- Verbally attacked someone for bringing you bad news or disagreeing with you (or members of your team)?
- Told a lie or been economical with the truth for purposes of deceit or personal gain?
- Claimed something on your CV or in an interview which was not true?
- Expressed views or opinions in order to 'fit in' with others around you? At a simple level this might be falsely claiming to be a cricket fan, but there are many other more serious claims.
- Bullied or harassed others (or made jokes at their expense)?
- Hogged the airtime on a Zoom call, Microsoft Teams call or in face-to-face meetings? (Think hard about this question and ask some of your colleagues – as we often take more time than we realise.)

- Been unwilling to share praise with colleagues or your team members?
- Shown a lack of respect to colleagues, team members or to your boss (either to their face or behind their back)?
- Asked for suggestions and then ignored all that were offered?
- Let colleagues (or the PR team) ghost-write social media content and then publish this in your name?
- Been intolerant or dismissive of other peoples' beliefs or views?
- Organised a brain-storming session where the most vocal person was you?
- Used your status or connections to get your own decision accepted?
- Told your boss (or your boss's boss) whatever you thought they wanted to hear, whether or not it was true?
- Pretended one of your team members was not promotion-ready rather than lose them from your team?

The more questions you agree with, then the less likely you are to be genuinely authentic. There are more questions we might add, but you have probably got the general idea by now. You might also like to think here about what behaviours or traits would make you regard someone else as being inauthentic or lacking in integrity?

What is authenticity?

How we define authenticity depends on different situations. At a personal level, it is about how you share information honestly and work collaboratively with others to build reciprocal relationships. Are you someone who people trust and can they rely on you?

There are occasions where we may be inauthentic. Such as pretending to be reasonably happy at work instead of being miserable – the difference being that our misery and gloom would impact on our colleagues. Even silent misery is noticeable and likely to spread quickly to others around us, as anyone who has had the misfortune to work with a gloomy colleague will recognise all too well. Another situation is joining a new company and taking the opportunity to leave behind some particular behaviour. For one person, working with new colleagues meant he was able to lose his stammer. For another who had lost a promotion contest, it meant they could move on without that personal failure remembered by all around them. In each case it was a clean start and a change made for positive reasons.

When we are seeking to understand what an authentic leader looks like, then it is likely to be a person with a strong moral compass. As psychologist Adrian Furnham outlines in *The Elephant in the Room*, the profile is also centred on honesty with high moral standards: a person who is ethical. (Ethical means that even if something is legal, it may not align with your values.) A person who is ethical has high self-awareness, feels comfortable to own weaknesses (as well as strengths) and is willing to share information and to self-disclose in an open and transparent way.

The impact of social media in recent years has created different challenges for leaders and authenticity. Research by two of the authors (Patricia and Viki) on this topic revealed some tensions and new expectations about leaders. One executive we interviewed, who was an 'early adopter' and innovator of social media in the health sector, highlights one problem:

'I had never had to share my private life or interests with my team members before, it wasn't part of my professional image as a manager. However, with social media I found it was essential to do this in order to establish my credibility with my followers and team members. At first, it was hard to do but gradually I found I could make the change, talking about football and films, family and well-being topics, and so added another important dimension to my leadership profile.'

This was not something he had needed to do before in his leadership role.

Research conducted in America by Simmons University (see Rivera-Beckstrom and Van Dam, 2021) asked conference delegates to identify what authenticity meant to them. From a range of open comments, the top three behaviours identified were as follows:

- honesty
- being open
- transparency.

In addition, the survey used the following statements (taken from academic literature as well as the researchers' own knowledge of authenticity) asking respondents to identify those which they believed exemplified authentic behaviour. The majority of respondents identified five key statements as shown below.

%	Statement
84	When I make a mistake, I own it and try to make things better.
81	I try to ensure that my actions have a positive impact on others.
78	I strive to tell the truth even if the news is bad.
72	I am able to act according to my personal values.
64	Who I am (my identity) aligns with how I present myself at work.

Reflection: How would you reply to these statements? Consider whether in your current situation you 'always' feel able to do this, 'mostly', only 'occasionally' or 'never' for each of the five statements. The first three set out below concern your own behaviours but the other two are centred on the workplace. For instance, how much freedom do you have in the workplace to be yourself? Was this different in a past job? While there might be diversity statements in your company along the lines of encouraging staff to 'bring your whole self to work', is that how you feel? Or do you (or colleagues) prefer to keep silent for whatever reason?

Personal behaviours:

When I make a mistake, I own it and try to make things better.

I try to ensure that my actions have a positive impact on others.

I strive to tell the truth even if the news is bad.

Work situation:

I am able to act according to my personal values

Who I am (my identity) aligns with how I present myself at work.

What are the implications of your answers to each of these statements?

Do you behave in an authentic way and if not, what could you do to improve this?

Can you be authentic in your workplace and if not, why not?

What are the main barriers or challenges which you believe are stopping you from doing this?

Understanding our values

Rarely do our personal values remain static. What we 'believe in' or value at the age of 20 is not necessarily the same by the time we are, say, 30 or 40, when we now perhaps have the added responsibilities for a young family and life partner or are caring for older parents. Some people may, for example, become more conventional and conservative with age; others take a journey in the opposite direction, becoming more rebellious and unconventional as they grow older.

A good deal has been said about the Millennial Generation and how important sustainability issues are for many of them. While this is a core value for Millennials (some of whom are now in their 40s) it resonates elsewhere with those in Generation Z and other age groups. Each will have certain values, ethical standards of behaviour and some 'no-go' zones; these are boundaries which cannot be crossed without compromising authenticity.

Similarly, your values may not be crystal clear and only come into sharp focus if a colleague, your company, team, family or a friend places you in a situation which compromises one or more of your core values. Here's an example: someone we know who was asked to give an excuse for his boss who is not joining an important meeting. The excuse was not true so should he do this? Truth may be an important value to him but still there are pragmatic considerations why he might make a compromise. Is he being too idealistic? What if, instead of passing on an excuse that might be called a white lie, he had been asked to pass on a tip for insider dealing? Can you appreciate that now the compromise will have to be much greater?

Often we meet people who join a company because its business purpose or values seemed congruent with their own. Many Generation Z people identify with corporate social responsibility and diversity issues. If there is disillusionment, then the person in question may feel trapped and so decide to leave. It is useful to consider your own core values and question whether they match the values of the business (and the boss) you currently work for. Chapter 7, which talks about social and emotional intelligence, may be helpful here, as this will provide you with a better understanding of yourself and your relationship skills.

By now we hope you have a better idea of your own authenticity so let's broaden this discussion to ask about the dynamics between yourself and others around you, both at home and at work. By this we mean how much space do you give others to be authentic? Do you respect their views and is there empathy and mutual respect between you?

Reflection: From the list below circle which of these values are important to you. You may prefer to create your own list of values.

▶

Your personal values	
A fair and just society	Integrity
Money and status	Compassion
Happiness	Truth
Political kudos and recognition	Justice
Service to others (or to the community)	Philanthropic and charitable causes
Tolerance	Respect for others
Intellectual capability	Ambition and career success
Sustainability and environmental issues	Honesty
	Helping others
Saving the planet	Competitiveness
Equality, diversity and inclusion principles	Perfection
	Add other values here which
Collaboration and cooperation	are important to you:

Have your values changed over the past few years and if so, why do you think this has happened?

Do your values align well with those espoused by your organisation? What about the values around you, among your colleagues and your boss? Are you compatible or incompatible on major issues or is there an authenticity gap? If so, what are the implications for you in the short as well as in the long term?

The power of mutual respect and empathy

Being truly authentic means you must also respect the views of others. You may sometimes notice a disconnect or gap, say, when certain people talk about 'respect' very energetically but then rarely apply this in practice. This sometimes becomes a surprising and uncomfortable 'reveal' in 360 Feedback sessions, when people hear such feedback from others around them. Lord Chris Patten, last Governor of Hong Kong and now Chancellor at the University of Oxford, was recently asked what he disliked most in others. His view, which is taken from many years at the top of politics, focusses on bad behaviour and lack of respect – '. . . the inability of people to imagine what they would feel like if others treated them as they behaved'. This same lack of empathy can also be observed in the business world.

So let's look a bit closer at the impact of lack of mutual respect and empathy. Firstly, think about people in your workplace and consider if some are not authentic. Think about your own behaviours, not only now but in the past. Have you ever rubbished a colleague's idea in a meeting or elsewhere in a public place, or encouraged members of your team to behave in a similar way?

There are two checklists below for you to work through. The left-hand column highlights what happens when empathy and mutual respect is missing. The right-hand column is the opposite scenario when empathy and mutual respect are present.

Empathy and mutual respect checklists: Have you observed any of these behaviours in your workplace? How do people generally behave? Mark those that apply.

When empathy and mutual respect are missing:	When empathy and mutual respect are present:
• Rudeness	• A curious mindset
• Lack of listening	• Genuine interest in the views and opinions of others, not only at a superficial level but much deeper as to 'walk a mile in their shoes'
• Lack of interest in others	
• Undervaluing people and making jokes at their expense	
• Elitist behaviours	• Creating dialogue and rapport
• Blinkered thinking	• Active listening and communication. Richard Fox in *Making Relationships Work at Work* describes this as 'listening heart and soul'; you need to listen intently to what others are saying
• Tolerance of inequality and unfairness	

▶

• Ignoring the feelings of some people (while being very protective about your own) • Sarcasm and critical comments targeted at people • Deliberately fault-finding and apportioning blame (a public shame and blame culture may exist in some teams and organisations) • Undermining the authority of others and/ or contradicting what they say, excluding them from various meetings or decisions • Treating people differently to other colleagues, e.g. with higher targets, lower or no privileges, limited or no salary increases and more problematic performance reviews • Unwillingness to speak out or call out about others who are disrespectful, rude and uncivil	• Self-reflection and self-questioning • Willingness to understand and challenge your own prejudices and potential bias • Being open-minded • You are inclusive rather than exclusive and while you are not necessarily sharing their principles you do understand these. In *Empathy* (2015) Roman Krznaric talks about the need to make an 'imaginative leap' into other people's shoes. More than any other it was this principle, the 'seeing is believing' experiential events, which inspired CEOs to get involved in The Prince's Trust in the UK. Founded by Prince Charles in the 1970s, The Trust became a catalyst between business and the most disadvantaged groups of society.
Impact: These behaviours will lead to a sterile atmosphere where people do not feel able to speak their mind, nor dare they speak truth to power; low levels of self-esteem; group think; flawed decision making; low morale, lack of creativity and innovation, lack of motivation and employee engagement; less effective team performance.	**Impact:** These behaviours are likely to create a high-energy buzz in a team or across an organisation. Sometimes this atmosphere is perceptible when you first join a team meeting. People feel valued and respected, their views are worthwhile and seen as adding value. While a hierarchy may exist in terms of seniority, age or experience this does not apply to intellectual debate.

Are these principles for developing empathy and mutual respect (those highlighted in the right-hand column) the default setting in your workplace, or for your team? Or are you more likely to encounter those highlighted in the left-hand column? When there are fireworks dealing with conflict, or a negotiating process breaks down or stalls, or a relationship begins to go awry, then it is usually because one or more of the guiding principles in the right-hand column above are missing.

A natural empath?

There also is the phenomenon of learned behaviours and in particular individuals who we would describe as 'fake empaths'. To explain, these people have learned the characteristics of empathetic behaviour and although they have absorbed every psychological feature, this is not their preferred behaviour – nor will it ever be. Instead, they have acquired this persona for particular reasons, to win promotion, popularity or other reasons. Many organisations, for instance, have a decided preference to nurture and appoint empathetic leaders. Outward appearances are often so seamless and sophisticated that this mask may deceive many, even those working closely with them and reporting to them.

Have you ever worked with a fake empath? A common description about such a person is one who is outwardly charming but utterly ruthless.

Conclusion

Never underestimate the power of authenticity. At both the personal and the business level it creates stronger connections between us. It is one of the most important aspects of that complicated psychological contract between individuals and those who employ us. Yes, of course we join a company to earn a salary; but there are emotional ties as well: we must respect our organisations and in return it must respect us. Anyone who has been trapped in a job where their values clash with those around them, or with those of their employer, will know just how difficult life can become.

There are good reasons why we are less authentic at different times in our career or in certain situations. Think of the young, inexperienced team leader who creates a jollier atmosphere in the team than they would prefer to do naturally. Or perhaps acts more confidently than they feel at heart. Both pieces of faux (or fake) authenticity would help bring a team together, creating a good team spirit. The team leader can later dial down on these assumed characteristics closer to their comfort zone, but that will still meet the needs of the team.

What we would encourage you to do is to check in with your current level of authenticity, to appreciate and value the principles of mutual respect. Also, reconnect with some of your values just in case you have lost sight of some of these in recent years. The more you understand the value of authenticity, mutual respect and empathy then the more likely you are to establish healthy work relationships.

The same principles will also help improve synergy with loved ones in your family and among friends! So, the next time someone (at work or at home) says 'you just don't understand me' or 'you're not listening to me', think about practising some empathy and mutual respect. Ask them to explain more about their views and hold back on being judgemental or dismissive. If it's at work, then ask someone such as your boss or a more experienced colleague to help you with this 'new' mindset. It can be difficult to stop doing what we've done for such a long time as it has been absorbed into what is often called our 'muscle memory'. This is our ability to learn and then be able to produce a particular behaviour almost without conscious thought – because with practice over time it simply becomes part of how we behave. An example of this is how we tell/teach our young children to be polite and to share (toys, sweets, etc.) with others and gradually this becomes a natural part of how they behave.

However, it can mean significant effort and change and reverting to previous established patterns of behaviour is one of the most typical challenges we hear about when we follow up on learning outcomes after an executive programme.

chapter 14

How to reset and improve a toxic relationship

'Relationships are based on four principles: respect, understanding, acceptance and appreciation.'

Mahatma Gandhi, lawyer, politician and activist

It is inevitable that alongside some good work relationships, there will be those that create problems and difficulties. Maybe all began well and has recently gone a bit sour or possibly you have inherited what has always been described as a challenging relationship. Whatever situation you currently have, the rest of this chapter will explore some reasons why this may happen and how using positive psychology can help you to move relationships from 'problems' to 'solutions' and to create a more appreciative workplace. This positive intervention can significantly improve a work relationship by creating a focus on ways to change attitudes and the dynamics of behaviour.

In particular we will consider the solution-focused approach. Much of this is about focussing clearly on what can help to reset and improve a relationship. It has been widely used both in teamwork and for personal work relationships. Rather than looking at what's gone wrong in the past, it looks to the future and how different ways of creating collaboration and synergy will improve the relationship.

First of all, though, let's take a look at some of those difficulties which contribute to rocky relationships. We've probably all experienced these at various times in our working life and it's worth highlighting a few of the typical issues we hear about.

What creates problems?

Sometimes problems with work relationships arise when a competitive element gets in the way. For instance, if two teams are vying to excel in terms of income generation (or for power or resources), instead of collaboration, the atmosphere resembles more closely a battle as they fight it out between them: one side will win, the other will lose. Similarly, we have certain key values such as the importance of integrity or a belief in hard work. And so it is likely to be more difficult to work well with someone who clearly does not share your work ethic and thinks it's more fun to fool around for some of the time. Lack of integrity is also a red line boundary to many who dislike dishonesty and Machiavellian behaviour, which exploits and manipulates anyone and everyone in order to achieve personal aims.

Another common experience is when there is a lack of trust by one person, or by all of those involved, which may be caused by a personality clash or any number of other reasons. There are of course certain people who thrive on creating problems and revel in upsetting those around them. Perhaps you can think of someone with this type of approach. If this is not unusual in the work environment around you currently, then you may be in a workplace which tolerates or even actively encourages ego-centric individuals as opposed to an ethos of sharing, collaboration and teamwork. It can be a toxic culture. By the way, you may belong to a 'team', but it can be filled with people who are self-absorbed and lack any willingness to share information. Where there is little in the way of mutual trust and respect, then the relationship is likely to be less than perfect – it is certainly unequal. Both these qualities of trust and respect are essential to achieve an outstanding work relationship. In the same way that you are likely to find that the best family connections are between individuals who trust and respect one another, the same is true in the workplace.

What else gets in the way of good work relationships? Quite a lot actually in terms of the organisational context. Just think about the increasing levels of complexity experienced business-wide over the past few years and the increased speed of response necessary to stay up to date within the sector, and in terms of meeting client demands. There also is the plethora of communication channels open to us at work both within the organisation and beyond those boundaries with our clients, suppliers, external partners and so on. This should in theory be an amazing tool as the speed, variety and intensity on offer provides more details than ever before, often 'in real time'. However, it is both a force for good and a force for bad, as many of us find that technology is not our slave but all too often is instead our master.

There is also the tricky question of how we communicate with each other. Take, for instance, the way we might quickly begin to blame each other for what's gone wrong rather than focussing on what to do to get things back on track. You accuse, the other person (or people) become defensive in their response and perhaps in turn are likely to attack and blame you. Once begun, a blame game can soon spiral out of control and tempers will fray. Hasty words may be said. How can you turn the focus from problem talk to solution focus and make your conversations more constructive and positive?

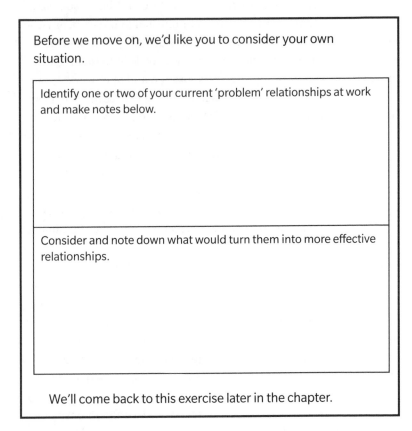

Before we move on, we'd like you to consider your own situation.

Identify one or two of your current 'problem' relationships at work and make notes below.

Consider and note down what would turn them into more effective relationships.

We'll come back to this exercise later in the chapter.

Moving to solution focus

We would like to show you how to turn damaged work relationships around by understanding and using the power of the solutions focus. SF was developed in the 1980s by a husband-and-wife team based in America, Steve de Shazer and Insoo Kim Berg. The couple, who had spent years working in family therapy, discovered that the most effective approach was to use what they now term the 'solution focus'. It involved two key elements as outlined below.

- What is it that a person is already doing that works and would help resolve the problem relationship? In other words find out what's working and build on this. Think, for instance, about times when a work relationship switches into a temporary good phase or there is a good day when all went well. Think about why this has happened and how this can be applied going forward. Finally, what needs to change in order to create a more positive work relationship?

- The second key element is to decide what the 'ideal' relationship would look like? Visualising a positive future is a simple way to show you what is possible. It is, if you prefer, what 'good' would look like. The aim is to identify what is important to you and what needs to change. If you have a bit of trouble at first imagining this, then think about how you might encourage more of what does work, say, when there has been a good phase in the work relationship. This will help you identify the key characteristics of the 'good phase' from when you have had a 'bad or rough phase' of that relationship. Then, knowing what change you want, what the ideal future looks like, you can more easily identify ways to build bridges and make stronger connections towards that future. It's as far away as possible from the antagonistic posturing, ego and rhetoric of blame games.

The solutions focus concept has been widely used in organisational change and coaching by Mark McKergow who has been involved in many projects with multinationals as well as with smaller family firms. The model is well tested and has been around for some 30 years now. It has been very effective in the organisational setting and much of its success comes from realising that pressing the pause button on a relationship, taking time to analyse the key issues and switch over to a positive frame of mind will enable change. It builds on strengths that already exist; these then need nurturing and coaching to help them flourish. You can achieve far more by changing your mindset about the way you think, the way that you behave and identifying ways to support others.

Asking yourself questions like those that follow will help you to refocus from problems to solutions:

- What would an ideal relationship look like?

- How do you need to change your mindset and behaviour in order to move towards that ideal future?

- What are the first signs likely to be that things are improving?

- What are the existing behaviours (or strengths) that you can build on?

It is important to think about small steps that will take you in the right direction. This is not about looking for a huge reorganisation of strategy or process or major change in personnel, resources or skill set. It's more about making small adjustments that lead to more constructive and positive conversations. You might also like to consider the following questions – as these can help identify key issues and challenges which we know from the research evidence often underlie toxic or problem work relationships:

- What level of respect and trust exists between the people involved?

- Do we appreciate each other's strengths and abilities, and do we take time to acknowledge these to one another? Mark McKergow talks about amplifying useful change by focussing on the behaviour which is working, elements that you want to encourage and develop further (Jackson and McKergow, 2007).

- How open, honest and transparent is communication (at all levels) with all of those who are involved?

- When we meet, do we fully focus on the key objectives of the discussion? Are key points summarised during and at the end of each meeting? Are people fully engaged in the debate and do they take ownership for the actions identified?

- Can we disagree in a healthy, positive way, without it escalating in confrontation?

So now, let's return to the earlier exercise in this chapter and focus more closely on one of those broken or difficult relationships.

Summarise the relationship you want to explore.

What could you do to bring out the best in the others involved?

What can you do to make a positive difference to that relationship?

It's all too easy with a problem relationship to focus on what's wrong with people. The SF approach is instead designed to help you concentrate on the positive and on yourself, although it can sometimes be hard to get started. An example of this happened with Ali, a team leader with an international team. Although it was a great team and they had won awards within the business, they relied heavily on his ideas and energy. He recognised this made the team too dependent upon him and that a model of shared leadership instead would create a more effective team. He decided therefore to leave space for others to contribute during team meetings. His usual style was to quickly dive in with a whole raft of 'ideas' which would then become the base for moving forward on whatever topic was under discussion. He knew this change would bring out the best in his co-workers, giving them time and space to contribute.

However, perhaps you can guess what happened in the first meeting when he applied his new approach. The energy levels sunk to near zero and, after a rather strange dysfunctional discussion with lots of silence, it was decided to postpone the discussion for a few days. Ali was at first mystified as to why people didn't open up with their ideas. Fortunately, as they left the meeting one of his colleagues confided to him that they didn't know what the purpose was of his strange behaviour. What was it all about? It was so unlike him not to dive in with suggestions and ideas.

Ali had assumed that simply leaving space in the regular team meeting would be sufficient, instead of letting his team know that he wanted to step back more in his style rather than continually leaping in too quickly with his ideas. They laughed about the misunderstanding and, once everyone was clear, the next meeting went so much better. Consider if you are changing your behaviour what the impact of this might be on others involved.

Preparing for more constructive conversations

For success in moving from problem focus – which most of us are very used to – towards solution focus, preparation is vital so that you can decide how you are going to adapt and flex your behaviour to enable more positive and constructive conversations. As illustrated by Ali's story above where he simply decided to change his way of operating, it is far more beneficial to spend some time to think things through and make a plan and decide how you will frame this for the others involved.

Consider the following areas when making changes to your usual patterns of behaviour:

- What your purpose and aims are?
- What is working well that you want to keep?

- What key processes and behaviours do you want to change?
- What common ground already exists?
- How will you know you are moving in the right direction?
- What would be an ideal outcome in this situation?
- What initial steps and actions will you take to set up the new ways of working to encourage more of a solution focus?

This preparation will mean that you are reviewing not only the 'what' but the 'how' of what is necessary to bring about a stronger connectivity and positive outcomes. Remember you are aiming for incremental change and it is always a two-way process where your own behavioural change models the sorts of behaviour and processes which will lead to greater mutual ownership, commitment and overall effective working practices.

Moving towards a more appreciative culture

By adopting the processes involved in solution focus and constructive conversations, you will be moving towards a more appreciative culture. An appreciative environment is created by encouraging people to be open, honest and respectful of each other and most importantly to develop the skill of using affirmative behaviour. In order to do this, you will have to work on your own listening and observation skills so that you are on the lookout for positive contributions. For instance, when you see someone doing something good or well then offer them some words of praise which will then encourage the person to use that behaviour more frequently. Go further than simply thanking them; in order to make others really appreciate what they are doing, tell them why the behaviour is working.

Building affirmative conversations into your day-to-day processes will quickly lead to a more positive and open work culture. The sort of thing you can do to encourage and model this is, for instance, at the end of a meeting ask others to say one thing they have enjoyed and found useful about the meeting. This sort of reflection is low risk but is beginning a process where you can introduce more reflection as people get used to this approach. Once they have grown accustomed to what they enjoyed about the meeting process, try asking them to turn to their neighbour and offer a positive affirmation about their contribution to the meeting. From there, the next stage might be to incorporate a positive and a developmental insight. By using this building blocks approach you are slowly creating new behaviours which build mutual openness, trust and respect and ultimately lead to a more appreciative culture.

Tips for moving working relationships from problems to solutions focus

- **It takes time** – Change is unlikely to happen quickly, so you need to be patient. Creating more effective work relationships is an art, not a science, so take your time and think about slow changes rather than immediate fast change happening. If your first idea does not work, that does not necessarily mean there will be no improvement: spend time considering what you might do instead.
- **Looking for the good** – If we look for negative aspects of behaviour then invariably we find them. Focus instead on positivity, developing a positive mindset to build on ways you can make a difference to the relationship. That does not mean of course that you have to become a doormat: in every work relationship you have rights as well as responsibilities.
- **Commitment** – You need to be committed to creating a more effective relationship, otherwise it will not work. If you undertake this reluctantly or don't have the patience to wait for change (as noted above), then little is likely to change.
- **Being more appreciative** – Build affirmative behaviours into all your interactions by focussing on what people are

doing well and telling them. Develop your skill of offering development feedback in a constructive way. Rather than just giving them the feedback, explain what you liked and why it made a difference; or, if it is more developmental feedback, then offer ideas for improvement.

chapter 15

—

Keeping your home/ work boundaries healthy

'**Your personal *boundaries* protect the inner core of your identity and your right to choices.**'

Gerard Manley Hopkins, poet and priest

Our relationships, both in and out of work, are fundamental building blocks of our lives, and we are familiar with that metaphor – of blocks being arranged together to form a structure, that structure being our very existence. However, the metaphor ends there. Building blocks are finite, with hard edges, and are held together with a definable substance, but our relationships are nothing like that. Much self-care literature today talks of the necessity for rigid, unbreakable, solid boundaries. The advice given is to be clear about your personal parameters – what you have energy for, what you have time for – and protect those boundaries at all costs. This, we are told will save us from burnout and preserve the authenticity of our real selves.

But, when we think of the word 'boundary' we think of limits, or frontiers, and when we cross one, we are in different territory, with different demands, rules and rewards, which usually require different behaviours from us. But in today's networked and hybrid working society, it is more and more difficult to be clear about where those frontiers lie. The boundary we are most used to talking about is the 'work/life' boundary, and what we mean by this is the line between our working life and our home life. But, of course, both those universes are not simple, but complex and interrelated.

Advice about boundary management often distinguishes between hard boundaries and soft boundaries. Hard boundaries are described as 'non-negotiables'. These are lines you are unprepared to cross: things you will not give up under any circumstances; things you will never do and things you will never accept. Soft boundaries are desirable but can be flexible, so might be hopes or aspirations – like trying to be in bed by 10.00 pm each night, but more often putting the light out at 10.30 or 10.45. Underpinning both types of boundaries are the permissions we allow ourselves and others. Permissions about what we will give and not give. For example, someone with a 'hard' alcohol boundary will never even have that 'just one small sip' of champagne at a wedding, but someone with a 'soft' alcohol boundary may join in the celebratory toasts with other guests.

Our relationship boundaries are to do with our need for healthy and fulfilling interactions with others. They determine the lines we draw for ourselves in terms of the permissions we give ourselves and others around our physical and psychological comfort when interacting with others. Relational boundaries can be emotional and/or physical, and can be related to our work, our home, our time or even our property. In fact, any time we are engaging or interacting with others we are invoking our own relational boundaries, and they are, of course, much more complex than our relationships with anything material.

Relational boundaries are designed to protect our self-identity, to separate us from some people and link us to others. Ultimately, they define our unique personalities and distinguish us from other people. It is important that we establish effective relational boundaries to ensure our relationships are strong, healthy and meet our needs. In effect, they are limits that we put in place to support our well-being.

Our relational boundaries touch every aspect of our life and can be physical, emotional, intellectual, communications related, or materials and financial.

- **Physical** – relating to contact or space with reference to your body and your tangible self as it exists in real space and time. For example, it may relate to how much touching or hugging we are comfortable with in public. Sexual boundaries are relevant here too. These refer to your expectations around physical intimacy: what is and isn't okay with you sexually. Much of the recent 'Me Too' movement has concerned violation of boundaries regarding personal space and physical identity, so this is clearly a topical and important area. Societal norms around preferences and expectations in this space have changed and are continuing to do so. It is therefore important to monitor our own, potentially dynamic, boundaries to preserve your well-being.

- **Emotional** – what we share, what we need and what we can give in the emotional 'space' are all determined by our personal relational boundaries. To establish them clearly, we need to understand and be honest about our feelings. Effective emotional boundaries are clear about what you need and what you are prepared to offer in your relationships. Effective emotional boundaries preserve the value and integrity of individuals, enabling them to operate autonomously, feeling attached and related to others but with a clear sense of 'self'.

- **Intellectual** – these boundaries cover our ideas and beliefs and perhaps our values and expectations. These boundaries, which govern the respect we show for our own and others' different views and ideas, are part of a tolerant and diverse society. Being afraid to share your views or opinions because of a fear or nervousness about the responses of others indicates a lack of psychological safety, and a lack of clear boundaries. This is often a really important area in our working relationships where our expertise, knowledge and skills are the currency with which we trade.

- **Communications related** – who we communicate with and how we send our 'messages'. They can relate to our rules of verbal communications such as not interrupting or swearing, or they can be more about non-verbal communications such as facial expressions of polite interest or eye contact. Communicating our relational boundaries is not always easy: misunderstandings abound, especially around sensitive issues, but the fact that they are difficult to communicate does not mean they don't exist.

- **Material and financial** – boundaries relating to our possessions and our property. These boundaries may be seen to be largely about money, but they relate to emotional issues around what money and material possessions represent, such as status, identity and success. Having different rules and agendas related to where and how you, your partner, colleagues and friends spend your money, or treat your possessions, can cause a great deal of strain on relationships.

To summarise, boundaries help relationships to function effectively. When you notice that you are feeling disrespected, taken advantage of, or hurt at work, you might want to consider how putting a boundary in place could improve this. Knowing and respecting your personal limits and needs can improve your working relationships and keep them healthy and strong.

When boundaries are clearly communicated, along with the consequences for breaking them, the other partners in your relationships can understand your expectations and you can work together to meet them. So how can we do that best at work?

What makes this difficult is that the distinction between hard and soft boundaries that we mentioned earlier is not always clear cut in working relationship boundaries. Working relationships are those that occur in our professional lives. These relationships take place between colleagues, clients and professional networks. However, the rise of social media, out-of-work bonding and virtual working means that the lines between personal and professional have become increasingly blurred.

Think of this real-life scenario as an example of this blurring of boundaries.

Jane works for a firm of solicitors in a large city and lives some 15 miles away in a country village. She loves her work and she and her husband socialise often with friends from the firm. She is part of a local school-run group where she is 'on duty' one week in four, and in those weeks, she uses her hybrid working allowance to work from home, working in the office full time for the other weeks. She has an elderly mother who requires transport to hospital appointments and shares this responsibility with her sister – a teacher in a secondary school in the city.

As well as relationships with immediate family, she also has multifaceted relationships with work colleagues and her local neighbours. There are clearly hard boundaries involved in managing a healthy work/life balance. A professional tone needs to be struck to meet organisational expectation, yet friendships involve a more casual and relaxed attitude. Friendships involve admitting vulnerabilities and weaknesses yet working

▶

environments may be less tolerant of these. Jane may need to set a soft boundary between the weaknesses she is happy to share and those she prefers to keep private, and of course, that soft boundary may shift as relationships and trust develop.

To develop trust, Jane could consider the key people in the groups and ask herself how much she has shared with them, or how they perceive the intricacies and interdependencies she is managing. Simple questions such as those below may create a better understanding of the situation and prompt the offering of new ways of coping with it.

- Are other people aware of the other responsibilities I have?
- How can I swap simple pieces of information between these different boundary groups in a way that might help when I am either trying to juggle too many balls in the air or simply running late? It has happened a few times recently.

This does not necessarily mean Jane telling everyone involved all the personal details of her life, but might allow others to offer creative solutions to their different bits of the 'puzzle'. It is hugely affirming to find that a boss, a colleague or a neighbour is happy to step in to ensure you can easily make another commitment. If they know what's going on for you, they may not only be happy to help, but will take great personal satisfaction from the interaction as well. This deepens relationships and creates trust – with many other benefits for all partners.

One of the ways Jane currently manages these intricacies is through several WhatsApp groups and Facebook pages. She is also, as required by her line manager, active on LinkedIn and Twitter. Establishing relational boundaries in situations like this is made more complicated firstly by the blurring of the emotional boundaries between work, family responsibilities and friendships but also by the blurring of the communications boundaries dictated by all the interconnections involved in the situation.

Does Jane's story resonate with you? While we are all familiar with the benefits and challenges that social media brings to our everyday lives, we are also realising that negotiating the boundaries between our professional and personal lives is an increasingly important part of our relational well-being.

Social media sites have revolutionised the way we communicate at work, with our networks offering broader reach than ever before. There are huge positives aligned with this, in terms of access to talent, markets and professional expertise. It is also true that activity on these sites can blur the boundaries between the professional and the personal, and we should carefully consider the potential impact on both our personal and professional lives.

We know that boundaries are important for healthy relationships, but most of us are less likely to create clear-cut borders for our online lives. Many people think that they don't need to set boundaries in the first place. We may, for example, go out of our way to help a colleague of a colleague with a recommendation on LinkedIn.

Psychologist and coach Dana Gionta (2016) argues that 'The most important reason to set boundaries online is for our personal safety and protection. Personally, you don't want to give out private information to the world, and professionally, you don't want to compromise your credibility and reputation'.

Gionta advises that whether you're using Facebook, Twitter, LinkedIn or any other social media website — or just writing email — you should ensure that you proceed thoughtfully with your time online. Here is her key advice on devising and defending your online boundaries.

1 **Give yourself permission.** Remember that we said earlier that boundaries are the permissions we allow ourselves and others in our interactions. Gionta supports this, suggesting that many people think that they don't deserve, or need, to set boundaries in the first place and so any boundaries that exist are wide, fluid and relatively ineffective. Good relational boundaries are controlled, managed and defended – we need to give ourselves permission to say 'No'.

2 **Consider your purpose.** Gionta is clear – setting boundaries needs forward thinking and planning.

Setting boundaries reflection

To help with this purposive planning there are some questions you can ask yourself.

- What do you want to get from social media?
- How would you like to use it?
- What purpose does social media serve for you?
- Are you using Facebook to keep in touch with friends, to network professionally or both?
- What would make you feel safe in terms of how many people you allow to be in your networks? Do you need an open or closed profile to meet your needs?'
- What kinds of information do you want out there?

---

3 **Set boundaries surrounding time.** We know this one is important. All social media sites can become intrusive and greedy of your time if you let them. It's easy to be seduced, especially if you're using social media sites professionally and want to build a network or supportive circle. The immediacy of the internet has created the expectation that we need to respond right away, so that we are continuously 'in the frame'.

But remember that you have a choice, and 'there is no requirement', Gionta said. Work out what is best for you according to the questions you have already answered here. How much time do you need to protect for social media? Be firm about the permissions you give yourself here – a hard boundary is usually appropriate.

Interacting with others

Gionta offers other tips for managing online relationships, which are summarised here.

- **Take things slow.** We sometimes think that the immediacy of the internet requires us to respond to relationships and communications more quickly than we would in a face-to-face relationship. Remember that it takes time to get to know people properly and this should be the same online. Online communications and relationships are rather one dimensional and so should be given more time to unfold and be trusted.

- **Ask for clarification.** It is so easy to misunderstand and misinterpret messages delivered online. We have no non-verbal communications except perhaps a small photo window. It is more important than ever in this space to check your understanding, ask for clarification and be sure you are all on the same page before you proceed.

- **Be honest about your feelings.** Be honest about your own and the other person's feelings. If you feel a boundary has been overstepped, it is easy to ignore if, for example, on a Zoom call. However, be careful to follow up later to avoid the difficulties festering into conflict. Sometimes, people just don't realise that they're crossing your boundaries and we can't always be sure we are crossing theirs. Keep in mind that everyone has different comfort levels.

At the end of the day, boundaries are about how something made *you* feel, so pay attention to your own emotions and comfort level – and respect those for yourself and for others.

- **Be thoughtful in your own responses.** When making or responding to comments, make sure you think through what you'd like to say, and consider how your message might be received. There are fewer opportunities online for recalibrating first, or incorrect, impressions. So, thoughtfulness becomes a key skill for creating effective working relationships.

The best way to establish workplace boundaries is to first set the tone in how you conduct yourself professionally – it should reflect the professional manner you hope others will return when engaging with you.

If you're looking for a way to set your own personal boundaries, it may be a good idea to complete the following table, as a way of thinking them through. You don't need to complete the whole thing in one go – start with what is most important to you.

Type of boundary	Hard/soft boundary	Purpose of boundary	What is acceptable from myself and others within my boundary	What is not acceptable from myself and others within my boundary	How to protect my boundary
Emotional (my feelings)					
Intellectual (my beliefs)					
My family relationships					
My working relationships					
Physical					
Online presence					

This chapter has been about how boundaries are important, but they aren't always easy to establish. We often don't know where to begin or how to communicate their needs to others.

The most important thing to remember is that we are all allowed, and indeed really need, to set these boundaries.

If we ignore our own needs for the comfort of others, we are not being safe. We risk burnout and stress through working at the edges of our resilience. It is very important for our well-being and for the well-being of our relationships at work that we understand our own parameters in terms of energy and capability. This is what allows us to perform at our best, and to help ourselves and our organisations to succeed.

chapter 16

Help: who can I turn to for support and advice?

'When I walk along with two others, from at least one I will be able to learn.'

Confucius

One of the most powerful tools for all of us is that we can achieve so much more if we seek help and support from others rather than working in isolation. You will sometimes hear this described as 'maximising your potential' which indeed it is. Learning from others is an amazing way to acquire new skills and behaviours, new attitudes and self-knowledge. Building agile relationships at work means that you have the skills and attitude necessary to change and evolve with others. Relationships, like the work environment, rarely stay static and, as they change, so too must the individuals involved.

In this chapter we will identify different ways you can seek help. There are no rigid rules about which option to try first nor an expectation to try all of these, though at the end of this chapter, 'If you change just one thing . . . ' offers you a single issue if you prefer this approach. However, you will gain most if you use a variety of options as all can offer valuable support and advice. Similarly, this idea of seeking help needs to remain with you throughout your career.

Value of learning from others

Not everybody recognises or wishes to acknowledge the value of learning from others. Sometimes there is a reluctance to seek help because some people make the mistake of confusing 'help' with 'remedial', thinking that seeking help is a sign of weakness as you are unable to manage without such help. To give an illustration of what we mean: a few years ago, one senior 'star' manager in mid-career was reluctant to try mentoring. This was because the general opinion across the company, and his own view, was that only ineffective individuals would require mentoring. Others, like him, who were already competent, outstanding team leaders would not need what they considered such basic help. Later, after being persuaded to join a successful mentoring scheme, he began to see how much he learned.

Not only could he see some of his overdone strengths, such as leaping forward instantly in every team discussion, but he spent more time reflecting on how he could become a better leader for those around him. We sometimes forget to note the impact our behaviour has on our co-workers. The mentoring also meant he appreciated different aspects of working with others, creating more effective agile work relationships. In other words, he was good before the mentoring, but the support made him even better. Those around him, including his boss, said he was more mature, more emotionally intelligent and far more aware of his impact upon those around him. He agreed, though before the mentoring began this was not something he was aware of. That kind of insulating mindset is not uncommon.

Just to be clear though, utilising and maximising such help is not an attempt to turn you into someone radically different to who you are now. Using these sources of help and support will broaden your understanding of your own behaviours and attitudes and therefore how best to use these to build and sustain agile relationships. Often, you have the opportunity to see a better, wider worldview than the one you have at present, which is an important reason why such support is valuable.

There is, or rather should be, organisational support available to help you build in better and more agile relationships. Every business should look closely at such issues to see not only what is happening but, most importantly, what can be improved. Consider for example the following two statements used in an earlier Ashridge Management Index survey that two of the authors (Viki and Fiona) were involved with. We asked nearly 1000 respondents involved in a variety of sectors and job roles about how easy it was to influence others in their organisation and about the support they received from the organisation to help them with virtual teams.

Building effective work relationships and organisational support

Statement	Respondents who either 'Strongly agree' or 'Agree' ($n = 987$)
Influencing people in my organisation is relatively easy to do	55%
My organisation provides sufficient support for virtual teamworking	45%

What do you think the results in your organisation would be? Would more people say it was relatively easy to influence others? True, the results above show us that the majority, just over half of those we surveyed, say this is easy but it is hardly an overwhelming vote of confidence. The level of agreement should be much higher at, say, 80 per cent or higher. Then, with regard to the second statement, how much support does your organisation provide for virtual team-working and is it enough? And here we mean that support is not just a few worthy policy statements but practical, innovative structures to help everyone improve the quality and effectiveness of virtual working relationships.

One general question worth asking yourself, and about the teams you are involved with, is how much help and support you currently receive. Think about the following as you should be able to answer 'yes' to at least one or more of these statements.

Who helps you build agile relationships?

I have a good boss who is willing to help and support me.
There is a circle of colleagues around me who are supportive in helping me build agile relationships.
I do have a mentor or coach.

Within the teams I belong to, or lead, there is support and help in building agile relationships – either this is from your own boss or others across the business.

My organisation offers various sources (or resources) of help and support for me and my co-workers to help us create good work relationships.

Examples might include: workshops on communications, collaboration and effective teamworking; executive education; mentoring or coaching programmes; teambuilding events; a comprehensive set of training options. We also would high-light that key training updates – such as for IT/technology issues – can add value, helping you to appreciate how to use technology in building effective work relationships.

Reflection: Now consider the sources of help which you currently use – whether within the organisation or those from external sources. Consider for each one how helpful it is – on a scale of 0 to 10 and make a few notes about how it has been helpful. Examples might include: regular team meetings, group workshops, advice and support from key individuals and so on.

Identifying current sources of help

Source of help you currently use	How helpful this has been (on a scale of 0 to 10, 10 = most helpful)	Notes about how this source has helped you

Once you have completed the assessment above look at those sources of help which you have scored highly, at 7 or 8 plus.

These are obviously valuable resources for you and so going forward it is important to keep these. You also might like to consider how you provide support and help for those you work with as this is a valuable approach which will help to create a more effective and efficient working environment. A number of people who are successful at a senior level use coaching to help their team as well as for themselves individually. But more about coaching in the next section of this chapter.

Let's take a look now about varying sources of help you can utilise.

Sources of help

In the figure below we have identified different sources of help and will briefly outline each of these in the following part of this chapter.

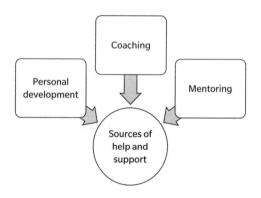

Key sources of help

Personal development

Whether or not we are aware of it, we all are likely to change over time. As we gain more experience most of us will acquire more skills so that the person who joins a team in two or three years' time becomes more effective and efficient simply because they are learning as they go along. Clearly, this is not a universal rule, but on the whole it is true. What is also true is that this process will work far better if you set yourself goals. For instance, if you want to improve collaboration with another team member then set out key steps.

1 Think explicitly about the best way to do that.

2 Discuss together what will make a difference, and why. Consider what your ultimate goal is.

3 Then, draw up an action plan to make sure the desired change happens. And make sure you focus on one, or at most, two targets. Otherwise, you are unlikely to achieve as much as you otherwise can do.

Always focus on **What?**, **Why?**, **When?** and **How?** to set new personal development targets. The same is true if you want to help someone else develop more agile work relationships. The more structure you create, the better you will create an action plan that will produce results – and with accountability. It's human nature: we all pay more attention if we are held accountable for what's likely to happen!

The value of **R and R** or 'Review and Reflect' is a great source of personal development. Finding different ways to review and reflect provides you with lots of opportunities for personal development. One practical and simple way is reflecting on the latest thinking in business journals (such as *Harvard Business Review*), recently published business books, podcasts and TED Talks. This might be focussed on key thinkers and business gurus or dealing with critical issues such as resilience, managing change and so on. The possibilities are endless.

If it's a need for ways to deal with work overload, then one of our recommendations is Daniel Levitin's *The Organized Mind* (2015). Finding ways to manage your information workload more effectively will have a direct impact on your working capability and therefore on how you are able to manage work relationships and collaborations. Setting aside a certain time, on a certain day each week will make it more likely that this then becomes a good habit in your working life. Some teams we know 'read and share' key articles with colleagues, and this has become a regular feature of team meetings.

Staying relevant: share (and read) together

Stop here and spend some time reflecting on who is in your network. Is it other techie people across the business who you can share with, or maybe you have a 'joined in the same year' group who keep in touch and stay close – even when they move on to other organisations? Simply factoring in a regular 'read and share' slot into regular conversations will help you all. And if you want to tap into personal learning among a group of people use the following prompts:

- What have you learned about your job/role recently and why might it be useful to others?
- Any particular challenge with regard to work relationships? How did you resolve this and would you do if something similar happens again?
- Tell us about a recent example of how you have helped others around you create more effective work relationships.

Coaching

Coaching is where someone – the coach – supports and guides you with different ways to develop more agile work relationships. If you already have a coach, consider if they could fulfil this role for you. Otherwise, find someone you trust and respect to be your coach. There is also the possibility of peer coaching where, together with a colleague you trust, you can develop an effective coaching relationship; perhaps you both work in the same part of the business or in neighbouring teams. Do remember though that a crucial part of such a deal should include confidentiality, so make sure this is discussed and agreed before you begin.

As with personal development mentioned above, if there are to be tangible outcomes rather than a broad brush of 'ideal' changes then remember to focus, focus, focus. Select something that needs to change and discuss how best to do this with the person who is coaching you. Make a commitment for a reasonable length of time with regular meetings between you both; check out what 'regular' means. To some people this might be weekly while others may have a very different, longer timescale in mind. You should expect any significant coaching assignment to last a few weeks or months as it will rarely be about instant results. It is much more about patiently working away at different ideas or approaches to create the right result.

Here are two examples where coaching works particularly well.

- Creating a more cohesive team environment and using coaching to help you find different ways to establish this with your co-workers. **TOP TIP:** make sure everyone in the team knows about the plan and can therefore play an active part in the process.

- Learning to 'let go' and delegate to others around you. **TOP TIPS:** plan ahead with this – to make sure you are comfortable with what will happen.
  Do not be discouraged if at first you find this creates stress. We know that delegation is a behaviour which some people find very hard to cultivate but stay with it and gradually you will see progress.

Remember, you are looking for a coach who will help you develop and grow. Someone who compliments you on every move you make may be great for confidence building but rarely moves you forward. Instead, it's worth remembering the words of the late Hilary Devey – she of the *Dragons' Den* TV series, and famous as one of Britain's outstanding female entrepreneurs. Filled with drive and determination herself, Hilary explained in an interview, 'I don't tolerate any nonsense and am often firm with my young protégés . . . You can kill with kindness, and my focus is on offering encouragement, constructive criticism, and a bucket-sized dose of reality'. You are looking for a coach who will challenge, encourage and be honest with you. Tough love.

Mentoring

Here the emphasis is a learning dyad or exchange system usually with someone more experienced than you. Possibly they have other skills you want to learn. One example is if the other person is already working successfully with remote teams or has an outstanding reputation in the business for being a change wizard or keeping important stakeholders onside (this last topic requires a very special skill set). Another is if you are about to move into an international appointment which the other person has held for a few years now. Who could be better? It is a perfect mentoring opportunity for an excellent transfer of knowledge, expertise and wisdom. The proviso of course is that they wish to share this knowledge with you, so beware of any such partnership where your mentor has been ordered to do this.

Again, as with coaching, it has to be a person who you respect, which is why we frequently find people keep mentors they meet early on in their career. Those people who help you then often become key figures throughout your career, and we regularly hear such stories from senior business leaders.

Some individuals believe that mentoring is for a short period of time. In truth the opposite is true: a great mentor is someone who you need to keep alongside you for the long term.

TOP TIP: think ahead about potential conflicts of interest. In some instances, this has happened when the boss is also the mentor. A plus point is that they are so close to you that they know the work environment and people around you well. Obviously, a fantastic learning opportunity, but there can be dangers. For example, if you want help about someone creating problems in your team, would your boss find it easy to stay impartial? What about your own plans? Could you, for instance, ask them to mentor you for a great promotion opportunity meaning that you were moving on somewhere else?

You might find the following book helpful for greater understanding of the two areas above: *The Leader's Guide to Coaching and Mentoring: How to Use Soft Skills to Get Hard Results*, Mike Brent and Fiona Elsa Dent.

Conclusion

Seeking help to build agile relationships offers valuable resources to develop your skillset at any stage in your career. It's often easy to pinpoint where you need help. Team relationships that you are involved with, for example, should be buzzing with energy and filled with people keen to create successful work. It's easy to spot when this is not happening by the way people describe the workplace environment, as with the staff in one business who recently said, 'team relationships here are built on fear, not on co-operation'. Clearly, that's a toxic environment to deal with, but whatever the situation, you don't have to manage all alone — there are a variety of sources of help that you can access.

If you change only one thing . . .

. . . then seek help to work on your own skills as changing yourself is always easier to do rather than trying to change other people around you. Consider the following questions:

- What skills do I currently have which help me build agile relationships?
- Do I constantly upgrade and improve these skills?
- Do I respect people as much as I should or could?
- What skills should I improve?
- What skills do I need in the future that I do not currently have? This question is particularly relevant if you are moving to a new role or taking on more responsibilities and complexities.

Stand at the shoulder of those people who excel at managing relationships and invariably you will find they either instinctively or through their own efforts have paid attention to focussing on those questions noted above. It is a skillset we can all acquire.

chapter 17

Frequently asked questions (FAQs): what we would do

What follows are a range of questions covering common themes related to working with others. Firstly, you might like to think how you might deal with each of these situations. We will then offer our suggestions.

The chart below lists a range of typical questions that are frequently posed when we are teaching, consulting and coaching. We suggest that, before we offer our ideas, you should give some thought and make notes about how you might deal with each of the scenarios.

Frequently asked questions
What would you do in this situation? Note down 3–4 ideas.

Q: How can I best influence my boss who only likes to hear solutions with as little detail as possible?

Q: One of my colleagues is always criticising the way I do things; I can't understand why. How do I deal with this?

Q: Most of my team are older than me and have been in the department for many years. They don't seem to want to explore the new ideas and ways of working that I have been brought in to introduce. How can I get them involved and more open minded?

Q: One of my team members is very techie oriented, not very emotionally intelligent and can divert team meetings by getting too involved in the detail. How can I deal with this?

Q: I lead a small project group and at recent meetings a couple of the group members have been very quiet and have hardly said a word. How can I encourage them to get more involved?

Q: My fellow teammates are men. Sometimes as the only female I feel rather marginalised and not included in day-to-day teamwork, online chats and conversations. What can I do to feel less marginalised?

Q: I have an opportunity to make an important presentation to one of our clients. Last time I had to present to clients I got very nervous and made a bit of a mess of it. How can I control my nerves and make more of an impact?

Q: It seems that some of my co-workers are playing games; telling me one thing and then not delivering on what has been promised. This has been going on for some time, but I don't know how best to deal with it. Help!

Q: In my part of the business we have someone who is a great organisational diplomat. They are always called in to cool things down when arguments and turf battles or too much ego clash, get too bad, and everyone knows that when they arrive, no matter how bad the situation is, that it will all be resolved. The last instance was a nasty row at board level where no one would back down. Our diplomat resolved the question calmly. It seems to most of us that such people are a strange mix of a strict headmaster, a kind honest friend to everybody and someone who immediately can pin down what's most important to fix. What are the skills that I need to learn to be that brilliant at 'Winning with Others'?

Q: The good news is that I have won promotion to another part of the business, but the bad news is my boss is someone with a terrible reputation as a bully. Everyone knows that this is true, but the senior team here will not admit it as she gets brilliant results for the business. How on earth am I going to cope with this as I certainly don't want to turn down this promotion as I may not get another opportunity? We have never worked together so all I know are the horror stories that are whispered 'in confidence' whenever the next person leaves her team! I'm tough but not sure that I'm Teflon coated enough for this boss; every previous boss has been a great person, more like a friend and mentor than someone ordering you around.
Or is this an example of challenging relationships?

►

> Q: I have just been given a major promotion. Until now I have been able to keep my work life in balance. However, in this new role I will have much more responsibility with a bigger team to manage and a multi-million budget to control. I have concerns that this will challenge my work/life balance. How can I ensure from the get-go that I do not become overwhelmed?

From our perspective

Q: How can I best influence my boss who only likes to hear solutions with as little detail as possible?

Knowing that your boss wants to be offered solutions is helpful and means that you should aim to offer your ideas early on in your influencing dialogue. Typically, someone with this preference is also interested in brevity and clarity. Start any influencing discussion with an overview of the issue followed by your suggested solutions and ideas. Then, pause and allow the boss to ask any questions or raise issues. This will then enable you to offer your rationale on how you got to these ideas. In other words, detailing how you came to these solutions/ideas – the process you used, who else was involved, the pros and cons and any questions or issues you are still thinking about. Remember to keep all of this brief, to the point and very clear. You should also expect questions and challenges along the way.

Remember, influencing is a process involving dialogue between people. To finish off you might like to offer the next steps or an action plan for the way ahead.

To read more about influencing see Chapter 9.

Q: One of my colleagues is always criticising the way I do things; I can't understand why. How do I deal with this?

First and importantly try not to take it personally. Criticism is usually aimed at work issues not at you personally. There are many reasons why people are critical, some of which can be to do with themselves and their personality type. Some people are naturally challenging and questioning in their approach to work and others can interpret this as criticism and take it to heart.

Start by thinking objectively about the criticism to determine whether there is any basis for it. This will give you time to process what the person has said and what your next move should be. Often the next step is to explore with the critical co-worker what the issue is and what he or she thinks you should do differently or how you might remedy the situation. Once you begin talking to the other person, it might be appropriate to inform them how you feel about the regular criticism – if it is regular. You might say something like, 'I'm feeling a bit puzzled as the last three or four times we have been in a discussion together you have criticised some aspect of how I approach my work. For instance: last week you . . . (describe what happened). . . '.

Then ask if you can talk about this with them. By using this approach, you may shed some light on why they criticise you and you may also help them to understand that, for instance, what they see as challenging you feel as criticism. It sometimes helps take the heat out of such a situation if you focus on asking for 'constructive criticism'. This means that you would like them to offer you a critique but also to offer constructive ways that the situation might be improved.

Above all try to stay professional and calm: that way you might learn from the situation and also build a better relationship with your colleague.

To read more about challenging relationships see Chapter 10.

Q: Most of my team are older than me and have been in the department for many years. They don't seem to want to explore the new ideas and ways of working that I have been brought in to introduce. How can I get them involved and more open minded?

This is a common issue that many people face and increasingly so with our ever more diverse workforce. Enthusiasm, new ideas and introducing streamlined work procedures are often reasons why people are appointed into a team leader role. By contrast, the team is often wary of change and if the team leader does not prepare their team members and pave the way effectively then it is highly likely that they will be fearful of, and reluctant to, accept change.

As a new team leader you might like to consider some of the following:

- Spend some time with each team member to find out about their role in the team: what they do and don't like about the work, what they are good and not so good at and any ideas they have for doing things differently that will be more effective.

- Once you know more about each person and their situation, feelings, views and ideas you can then begin to gather your thoughts and begin planning how you might move ahead.

- Think about the new ideas and work procedures you want to introduce and with what you now know about your team members ask yourself:

  ○ Which ones will be easiest to introduce to your team members?

  ○ Which ones will be the most difficult for your team to accept?

  ○ Which ones will have the most impact on the work?

  ○ Which ones will be most beneficial for the department/organisation?

- This information should help you to prioritise the ideas and decide which ones to start with, how you will introduce them, your timeline and how you will review the changes with your team.

The keys to bringing in any change are to listen to your people, involve them in the process, start with the less contentious changes and above all have patience. Remember to do regular updates and progress reports in team meetings, and above all to explain why the change will be beneficial to the team.

To read more about authenticity, respect and empathy see Chapter 13.

Q: One of my team members is very techie oriented, not very emotionally intelligent and can divert team meetings by getting too involved in the detail. How can I deal with this?

People who possess expertise in an area of their work as well as being less socially aware than others can indeed misread what is going on in team meetings. Many of these people are unaware of the impact they have on others during meetings. It is often their own need to fully understand all the data and processes that are driving their behaviour.

You might like to try having a pre-meeting with this person to headline the purpose and content, thus giving them time to think things through beforehand and to come back to you with any detailed questions. Or, at the outset of the meeting make the point that this is a general information-giving meeting and does not require lots of detail at this stage. Also you can offer people the opportunity to talk with you post meeting about any issues that are unresolved for them. By doing this you are giving yourself permission to interrupt anyone who goes into too much detail and suggesting that they take this offline and discuss later.

You might also wish to share with the person the impact of their behaviour on yourself and others in the meetings and then explore with them ways of operating that meet both their and your needs.

To read more about social and emotional intelligence see Chapter 7.

Q: I lead a small project group and at recent meetings a couple of the group members have been very quiet and have hardly said a word. How can I encourage them to get more involved?

In any group of people everyone is unique with different personalities, needs and wants. Each person will behave differently – some will be quiet and reflective, others will be extrovert and chatty, others questioning and challenging and many other behaviours. One thing to be aware of is that for some people their approach is to observe, listen and measure the lie of the land before pitching in and getting involved.

One approach is to involve the quieter people by asking for their thoughts. Perhaps by saying something like – '(Person's name) . . . It would be great to have your ideas about this project, so what are your thoughts?' or '(Person's name) . . . You have some experience in this area, what do you think? What are your first impressions or are there some questions that we have not yet asked about this?'

Another way of doing this is to say at the start of the meeting that you'd like to hear from everyone during the meeting about the issues being discussed. That way all participants are pre-warned that you may ask them a question especially if they don't offer a thought. It will also give people who are naturally quieter thinking time to plan what they want to say.

A technique we find very successful in encouraging involvement from everyone is to use the following process:

- Prior to the meeting set and share your agenda.

- Be very clear about the objective and desired outcomes, i.e. an action plan for the way ahead.

- Give people warning that you expect them to come along to the meeting willing and able to share their thoughts and ideas about the topic/objective. This is a collaborative meeting where everyone will be required to contribute. Encourage innovation, creativity and new ideas.

- At the meeting restate your objective and explain the process you wish to adopt:

  ○ The time available for the meeting.

  ○ Agree who will manage the time and be the scribe. (Often best if this is an outside facilitator – some other person not involved in the process.)

  ○ First 30/40 minutes is allocated for sharing and capturing everyone's views and ideas. Everyone has between three and five minutes uninterrupted to share their ideas and thoughts

with the whole group. Timing depends upon the number of
people in attendance and the time available.

- ○ 30/40 minutes for analysing, synthesising and making
  meaning of what has been shared – i.e. testing understanding
  for clarification but still not judging.

- ○ Remaining time allocated to evaluating and developing the
  ideas together with a way ahead, next steps and any action
  plans.

Rules for the meeting:

- During the sharing phase each person will have an equal portion of
  time allocated to share their ideas and thoughts about the topic –
  usually between three and five minutes. Be ruthless with time;
  that is, no one overruns!

- During that time there will be no interruptions or judgements –
  all you must do is listen.

- Once everyone has shared their ideas, begin the process of
  analysing and synthesising what you have heard to develop and
  identify the way ahead, next steps and any appropriate action
  plan – we all have different ways of doing this. At this stage the
  project owner takes the chair and manages the process.

**To read more about diversity, inclusion and inclusivity see
Chapter 8.**

**Q: My fellow teammates are men. Sometimes as the only
female I feel rather marginalised and not included in day-to-day
teamwork, online chats and conversations. What can I do to feel
less marginalised?**

Firstly, be clear in your own mind about what it is that they do that
makes you feel marginalised. Also, reflect about why you are feeling
marginalised, what the impact of it is on you personally and on the
work of the team. In situations like this, clarity about the issue is vital.

In our view one of the best ways of dealing with this sort of
gender issue is to call it out. So, next time something happens that

you feel leaves you out of the loop tell your fellow teammates and explain how this makes you feel. However, beware that this does not create a negative response if your colleagues did not mean to exclude you.

Another approach that is often effective and non-confrontational is to find one person in your team who you are happy to share this with. You must speak to someone who will support you; do not leave this kind of situation to continue. Once you have someone as an ally to help you then invariably life will become more pleasant and inclusive; that person, for example, will directly say to others 'oh, we haven't included x' so that you don't need to pitch in with 'I feel I'm being left out . . . again'.

Some organisations where diversity issues have been considered in more detail often find it helpful to provide a buddy or friend for those people in a minority.

To read more about diversity, inclusion and inclusivity see Chapter 8.

Q: I have an opportunity to make an important presentation to one of our clients. Last time I had to present to clients I got very nervous and made a bit of a mess of it. How can I control my nerves and make more of an impact?

When presenting to any audience the main keys to confidence and impact are preparation and planning. So:

- Make sure you know the overall objective or purpose of the presentation.

- Thoroughly familiarise yourself with the material about the topic. Make sure you focus on quality content and do not continually repeat certain sections as this is a common error at every level of business.

- Know your audience – who they are and their expectations.

- Anticipate questions and think about how you might answer them. If it's possible try to have a friendly question at the beginning.

- Keep any notes short – more as prompts. If you are well prepared and know your subject all you will need is gentle reminders.

- Any visual aids should add value to your words not simply repeating what is on the screen.

- If you are using any technology familiarise yourself with it prior to the presentation to be sure you know how it works and familiarise yourself with the room layout.
  If things should go wrong, then keep a cool head. Don't let it show that it has knocked you for six. We often hear that a person who can be clear thinking in such a situation wins their audience over. You have to continue to speak to the audience. Remain practical in thinking through how to solve the issue as this will impress your audience as in the examples below.

In one instance we recently heard about how the planned technology was not used by the organisation where the presentation was held. Think about what you would do if all your technology plans fail. How will you make a presentation if that should happen? In this case the person was unfazed and spent a busy ten minutes at the front of the room to find different ways to transfer files so that they could then be used.

Be prepared: in another instance at a major European conference there was an electricity outage. Most presenters were at a total loss about how to deal with this and some workshops were cancelled. Only a few people had the forethought to have a printed summary of their presentation.

- From an impact perspective think about what you are going to wear – be smart and comfortable. Think about your body language – stance, gestures, facial expressions, eye contact – all should be natural and remember to smile and look at your audience especially when you introduce yourself.

- Your voice should be varied – highlighting key points by using a pause and slight raise of the voice. Vary both your intonation and pace for interest and impact.

- Indicate at the start when you would like to take questions – nothing throws you off balance more than being constantly interrupted. Think ahead about how you might deal with the situation if the questions are challenging.

- If your presentation is cut short – for whatever reason – make sure you have a clear idea of one or two key points that are essential to your message.

Also, recognise that nerves before a presentation are normal. Very few people don't experience nerves – they contribute to the adrenalin that drives our performance: it's all about channelling the nerves by doing your homework and being well prepared.

Practice is also important – whether it's rehearsing for an important presentation or taking the opportunity to present to an audience as often as you can nothing improves your performance and impact more than getting out there and doing it.

To read more about maximising personal impact and impression management see Chapter 11.

Q: It seems that some of my co-workers are playing games; telling me one thing and then not delivering on what has been promised. This has been going on for some time, but I don't know how best to deal with it. Help!

This is largely an issue of relationship awareness and building trust. Firstly, recognising that this is an issue and identifying the protagonists is a good starting point. Once you know who you are dealing with you can begin to plan how best to deal with the individuals concerned and to mitigate against similar games happening in the future. Start by reflecting about the quality of the relationship you have with each of the individuals – you could use the relationship awareness model in Chapter 10 to help you with this. This will then help you to think through the best approach/es to take – there may be different ones for each person.

Depending upon the actual individual you might like to try some of the following:

- When you ask someone to deliver something try setting a review date when you can meet to review progress and plan the next steps.
- Keep regular contact with these people by checking in as to how things are going and asking questions about progress, and so forth. . .

- You could offer feedback to an individual about their behaviour and the impact it has on you. This then could lead to a discussion about how you could work together more effectively.

- As a last resort you could call someone out. This is very direct and can appear combative but with some people this sort of approach can be most effective.

Remember it is most important to tailor how you deal with each person individually. No one approach suits everyone.

To read more about relationship awareness and trust see Chapters 4 and 6.

Q: In my part of the business we have someone who is a great organisational diplomat. They are always called in to cool things down when arguments, turf battles or too much ego clash, get too bad, and everyone knows that when they arrive, no matter how bad the situation is, it will all be resolved. The last instance was a nasty row at board level where no one would back down. Our diplomat resolved the situation calmly. It seems to most of us that such people are a strange mix of a strict headmaster, a kind honest friend to everybody and someone who immediately can pin down what's most important to fix. What are the skills that I need to learn to be that brilliant at 'Winning with Others'?

People like this are rare indeed. There are a few key elements that contribute to this – the individual's personality, their skills (interpersonal, relationship and leadership), the person's level of self-confidence and their position in the organisation.

Let's focus on the skills that you might want to focus on:

- Influencing and persuading others – understanding the process and skills involved in influencing others effectively. **(See Chapter 9.)**

- Social and emotional intelligence – a good understanding of this area will help you to build your self-awareness, self-confidence, self-control and social skills. **(See Chapter 7.)**

- Conflict resolution – understanding the characteristics of conflict in the workplace and how to deal with it. **(See Chapter 10.)**

- Building trusting relationships – having a reputation as someone who can be trusted and who is open, honest and reliable. **(See Chapter 6.)**

- Excellent communication skills – enabling you to talk through issues to build shared understanding and meaning. **(See Chapter 12.)**

- Focussing on solutions – instead of dealing with things as problems and looking at what's gone wrong in the past look to the future and think about how you can improve the relationship. **(See Chapter 14.)**

These are some of the major skills that will set you on the track to become an organisational diplomat. However, this whole book is written to help people develop their relationship skills and reputation.

Q: The good news is that I have won promotion to another part of the business, but the bad news is my new boss is someone with a terrible reputation as a bully. Everyone knows that this is true, but the senior team here will not admit it as she gets brilliant results for the business. How on earth am I going to cope with this as I certainly don't want to turn down this promotion as I may not get another opportunity? We have never worked together so all I know are the horror stories that are whispered 'in confidence' whenever the next person leaves her team! I'm tough but not sure that I'm Teflon coated enough for this boss; every previous boss has been a great person, more like a friend and mentor than someone ordering you around.

Bullies are notoriously difficult to deal with and especially if they are in senior roles and deliver on their performance targets. However, there are some things you can do to protect yourself and to get your relationship off on a firm footing.

First of all, keep an open mind and start the relationship by discussing with your new boss how they like to work as well as sharing with them how you like to work. I'm guessing the person was involved in the promotion decision so from that perspective they must be impressed with your work and your potential. You never know you may find that the 'bullying' is more about being tough on performance!

If, however, it does turn out that the boss is a bully try to identify how the bullying behaviour manifests itself. Typically bullies use a range of behaviours including:

- aggression – language, shouting, emails, body language, picking on people in front of others

- hypocrisy – someone who double deals, talks behind your back and undermines you

- being overly critical – someone who is never happy with your achievements and constantly chips away at your self-confidence

- the manipulator – a person who negatively influences you by affecting your mental and emotional well-being for instance by playing mind games, making you feel guilty, blaming you or telling lies and excluding people from certain work activities.

When you know the type of bully you are dealing with you will have a clearer idea of how you might deal with the person.

Some of the things you can try are:

- Deal with it early in the relationship, don't let it go; if you ignore it then it will only get worse. Nip it in the bud by explaining what they did that made you feel uncomfortable and how it is affecting your work. Suggest how you might work better together in the future. The most important thing here is to stay calm, rational and professional.

- Document any bullying that occurs – keep a journal of who's involved, when it happened, what and why you think it happened. It's important to have evidence for when you feel able to deal with it.

- Once you get to know your colleagues you might like to share your experiences with those people who you believe are also being bullied. Perhaps you can join forces to tackle the bully en masse by pointing out how their behaviour is affecting the work and emotions of the team.

- Talk to someone in your HR department by focussing on how it's affecting people's behaviour and performance.

- Talk to someone more senior who you trust to see if they can help.

If you have tried to deal with the bully and have not succeeded in effecting change then the important thing about bullying is to know when to leave it alone and to look for ways to move on.

To read more about tricky relationships see Chapters 5 and 10.

Q: I have just been given a major promotion. Until now I have been able to keep my work life in balance. However, in this new role I will have much more responsibility with a bigger team to manage and a multi-million budget to control. I have concerns that this will challenge my work/life balance. How can I ensure from the get-go that I do not become overwhelmed?

When anyone gets a promotion, it can be a challenge for their work/life balance. One hopes that the challenge is a short-term one because you can put certain checks and balances in place to ensure things do not get out of hand. Some of these things are:

- In the early days of any promotion spend time categorising the various elements of the job – as a starter you could use the must/should/could categories. This will give you an overview of the new role broken down into manageable chunks.

- Once you have a clear idea of the full range of responsibilities you can begin to identify those parts of the job that require your full attention, those that can be delegated or are the responsibility of your team. The challenge here is to remember that you are in a new job and there will be elements of this that you find easy and like doing, find difficult, challenging, are new to you and are key elements of the new role. You have to be selective and make sure that you dedicate your time to the tasks that are high priority and contribute to your success in the role.

- Start as you mean to go on. By that we mean set parameters around your working practices especially the hours you put in. This is vital so that you can allocate sufficient time to your personal life – family, friends, hobbies, fitness and social life and so on. . .

- Draw a line between work and home life and try not to bring work issues home with you.

- Get to know your new boss by spending time together so that you are clear about their expectations of you and so that they under-stand how you want to work.

- Identify people who can support you, mentor you and maybe even challenge you. When you take on a new job it is important to get to know the people around you and those you would like to have in your network and the role they might play.

To read more about managing work/home boundaries see Chapter 15.

References and further reading

Argyris, C. (1990) *Overcoming Organizational Defenses: Facilitating organizational learning,* 1st edn. Pearson Education, Inc.

Bailey, S. and Black, O. (2014) *MindGym: Achieve more by thinking differently.* HarperCollins.

BBC Radio 4 (2021) *Fortunately . . . with Fi and Jane.* 2 July, Programme no. 196.

Berne, E. (1964) *Games People Play: The psychology of human relationships.* Penguin Books.

Bird, P. (2011) The ARC of Distortion. 23 April. ProjectSmart. Available at: https://www.projectsmart.co.uk/communications-management/the-arc-of-distortion.php

Bohm, D. (2004) *On Dialogue.* Routledge.

Bourke, J. and Titus, A. (2020) The key to inclusive leadership. *Harvard Business Review,* 6 March.

Branson, R. (2008) *Business Stripped Bare.* Virgin Books.

Branson, R. (2014) *The Virgin Way: How to listen, learn and lead.* Virgin Books.

Brent, M. and Dent, F.E. (2010) *The Leader's Guide to Influence: How to use soft skills to get hard results.* FT Publishing.

Brent, M. and Dent, F.E. (2014) *The Leader's Guide to Managing People: How to use soft skills to get hard results.* FT Publishing.

Brent, M. and McKergow, M. (2009) No more heroes. *Coaching at Work,* 4(5).

Clarke, J. and Nicholson, J. (2010) *Resilience: Bounce back from whatever life throws at you.* Crimson Publishing.

Costa, P.T., Jr and McCrae, R.R. (1998) Trait theories of personality. In D.F. Barone, M. Hersen, and V.B. Van Hasselt (eds) *Advanced Personality* (pp. 103–121). Plenum Press.

Coutu, D.L. (2003) *Harvard Business Review on Building Personal and Organisational Resilience.* Harvard Business Review Press.

Covey, S.M.R. and Merrill, R.R. (2006) *The Speed of Trust: The one thing that changes everything.* Free Press.

Dawkins, R. (1976) *The Selfish Gene.* Oxford University Press.

Davda, A. (2012) *How to improve your personal resilience.* Public Finance.

Davda, A. (2017) *Ashridge resilience questionnaire.* Ashridge Psychometrics.

Degner, K. (2021) *Guide to Virtual Team Building – 55 Team Building Activities to Improve Communication, Build Trust and Boost Morale in your Remote Team.* Independently published.

Dent, F. Ashridge Psychometrics – The Influencing Style Preferences Inventory.

Dent, F.E. (2009) *Working Relationships Pocketbook.* Management Pocketbooks.

Dent, F.E. and Brent, M. (2006) *Influencing: Skills and techniques for business success.* Palgrave.

Dent, F.E. and Davda, A. (n.d.) ISPI. Available from Ashridge Executive Education.

de Shazer, S. and Dolan, Y. (2008) *More Than Miracles: The state of the art of solution-focused brief therapy.* Routledge.

Dhawan, E. (2021) *Digital Body Language: How to build trust and connection no matter the distance.* HarperCollins.

Drayton, M. (2021) *Anti-burnout: How to create a psychologically safe and high-performance organisation.* Routledge.

Edelman (2021) *Edelman Trust Barometer.* Edelman Inc. See www. edelman.com.

Ekman, P. (2004) *Emotions Revealed: Understanding faces and feelings.* Weidenfeld & Nicolson.

Fleming, K. (2016) *The Leader's Guide to Emotional Agility: Using soft skills to get hard results.* FT Publishing.

Fosslien, L. and West Duffy, M. (2019) *No Hard Feelings: The secret power of embracing emotions at work.* Portfolio.

Fox, R. (2020) *Making Relationships Work at Work: A toolkit for getting more done with less stress.* Practical Inspiration.

Furnham, A. (2007) *The Elephant in the Room: The causes of leadership derailment.* Palgrave Macmillan.

Gardner, H. (1983). *Frames of Mind: The theory of multiple intelligences.* New York, Basic Books.

Gault, T. (2008) Advocacy and inquiry. *EzineArticles.* See https:// ezinearticles.com/?Advocacy-and-Inquiry&id=1091768.

George, B. (2015) *Discover your True North: Becoming an authentic leader.* Wiley.

Gionta, D. (2016) See https://psychcentral.com/lib/10-tips-for-setting-boundaries-online#1

Goleman, D. (1995). *Emotional Intelligence.* Bantam Books, Inc.

Grant, A. (2020) TED Talk, Burnout is Everyone's Problem. See WorkLife with Adam Grant: Burnout is everyone's problem | TED Talk.

Harvard Business Review (2003) *On Building Personal and Organisational Resilience.* HBS Press.

Harvey, E. and Taylor, T. (2019) *Respect in the Workplace: You have to give it to get it.* WalkTheTalk.com.

Hassan, O. (2016) *Influencing Virtual Teams: 17 tactics that get things done with your remote employees.* CreateSpace Independent Publishing Platform.

Hasson G. and Hadfield, S. (2009) *Bounce: Use the power of resilience to live the life you want.* Pearson.

Hasson, G. (2014) *How to Deal with Difficult People: Smart tactics for overcoming the problem people in your life.* Capstone.

Hello Magazine (2013) 'Dragons' Den' star Hilary Devey on business success and personal regrets. 2 April.

Hill, A. and Jacobs, E. (2021) Graduate jobs after the pandemic: 'I'm only an email address to my team'. *Financial Times,* 4 July.

Hind, P. and Holton, V. (2019) The changing nature of leadership: an exploratory investigation into how the evolution of social media is changing what it means to be an effective leader. Research Report for UNICON, Consortium for University Based Executive Education. UNICON.

Hume, N. (2021) FT profile: The measured man shaking up the world's biggest Miner by Neil Hume. *The Financial Times Weekend* 21/22 August.

Jackson, P.Z. and McKergow, M. (2007) *The Solutions Focus: Making coaching and change simple,* 2nd edition. Nicholas Brealey Publishing.

James, O. (2013) *Office Politics: How to thrive in a world of lying, backstabbing and dirty tricks.* Vermilion.

John, O.P. and Srivastava, S. (1999). The Big Five Trait taxonomy: History, measurement, and theoretical perspectives. In L.A. Pervin and O.P. John (eds) *Handbook of Personality: Theory and research* (pp. 102–138). Guilford Press.

Jones, P., Van Hool, J. and Hailstone, P. (2004) *Impact & Presence Pocketbook.* Management Pocketbooks.

Kim, W.C. and Mauborgne, R. (2003) Fair process: managing in the knowledge economy. *Harvard Business Review,* January.

Kim, W.C. and Mauborgne, R. (2005) Value innovation: a leap into the blue ocean. *Journal of Business Research,* 26(4).

Kramer, L. and Barrera, I. (2008) *Using Skilled Dialogue to Transform Challenging Interactions.* Brookes Publishing Company.

Krznaric, R. (2015) *Empathy: Why it matters, and how to get it.* Rider.

Lencioni, P. (2005) *Overcoming the Five Dysfunctions of a Team.* Jossey-Bass.

Levitin, D. (2015) *The Organized Mind: The science of preventing overload, increasing productivity and restoring your focus.* Penguin.

Loehlin, J.C., McCrae, R.R., Costa, P.T. and John, O.P. (1998) Heritabilities of common and measure-specific components of the big five personality factors. *Journal of Research in Personality,* 32(4), 431–453. https://doi.org/10.1006/jrpe.1998

McArthur, J.A. (2016) *Digital Proxemics: How technology shapes the ways we move.* Peter Lang.

Maslow, A. (1943) A Theory of Human Motivation. *Psychological Review,* 50(4), 370–396.

Matuson, R.C. (2021) *Seven Principles for Managing Difficult Conversations at Work.* Kogan Page.

Miller Coles, B. (2020) 8 top tips for improving your body language during virtual meetings. *Forbes,* 17 September.

Morgan, N. (2018) *Can you Hear Me? How to connect with people in a virtual world.* Harvard Business Review Press.

Murray, K. (2020) *Charismatic Leadership: The skills you can learn to motivate high performance in others.* Kogan Page.

New York Times (2016) What Google learned from its quest to build the perfect team. 28 February. Available at: https://www.nytimes.com/2016/02/28/magazine/what-google-learned-from-its-quest-to-build-the-perfect-team.html

Osborne, C. (2002) *Dealing with Difficult People.* Dorling Kindersley.

Osland, S., Kolb, D.A. and Rubin, I.M. (2000) *Organizational Behaviour: An experiential approach,* 7th edition. Pearson.

Pease, B. and Pease, A. (2017) *The Definitive Book of Body Language.* Orion.

Perel, E. (2019) Esther Perel on Relationship Skills and Workplace Dynamics at SXSW 2019. SXSW. Available at: https://www.sxsw.com/interactive/2019/esther-perel-on-relationship-skills-and-workplace-dynamics-at-sxsw-2019-video/

Postma, N. (2021) You can't sit out office politics. *Harvard Business Review,* 14 July.

Rai, M. (2020) *The Values Compass: What 101 countries teach us about purpose, life and leadership.* Nicholas Brealey.

Rath, T. and Clifton, D.O. (2004). *How Full Is Your Bucket? Positive strategies for work and life.* Gallup Press.

Reina, D.S. and Reina, M.L. (2010) *Rebuilding Trust in the Workplace: Seven steps to renew confidence, commitment and energy.* Berrett-Koehler Publishers.

Remen, R.N. (1996) *Kitchen Table Wisdom: Stories that heal.* Riverhead Books.

Rivera-Beckstrom, A. and Van Dam, E. (2021) *The Importance of Authenticity in the Workplace: The 2021 Leadership Development Survey.* Simmons University Institute for Inclusive Leadership.

Saj-nicole, J. and Beyer, D. (2010) *The Right Fight: How great leaders use healthy conflict to drive performance, innovation and value.* HarperBus.

Seligman, M. (2018) *Learned Optimism: How to change your mind and your life.* Nicholas Brealey Publishing.

Senge, P.M. (2014) *The Fifth Discipline Fieldbook: Strategies and tools for building a learning organization.* Crown Business.

Shaw, G. (2020) *Bold Body Language: Win every day with nonverbal communications secrets.* Communication Excellence.

Shulman, A. (2016) *Inside Vogue: My diary of Vogue's 100th year.* Fig Tree.

Sinha, R. (2021) New to the team? Here's how to build trust remotely. *Harvard Business Review,* 23 March.

Tyler, R. (2022) Mentors needed to deliver Sunak's business training. *The Times,* 23 May.

Velsor, E.V. and Leslie, J.B. (1995) Why executives derail: perspectives across time and cultures. *Academy of Management Executive* (1993–2005) 9(4).

Waldman, J. and Jackson, P.Z. (2017) *The Resilience Pocketbook.* Management Pocketbooks.

Webb, L. (2013) *Resilience: How to cope when everything around you keeps changing.* Capstone Publishing.

Weiss, J. (2016) *HBR Guide to Negotiating.* Harvard Business Review Press.

Wilkins, A. (2018) *Change and Opportunity: How to lead and manage change in seven key steps.* Perspectiv LLP.

Index